KETO CHAFFLE RECIPES #2020

90+ Of The Most Irresistible Ketogenic Low Carb Chaffles To Boost Metabolism, Weight Loss, And Fat Burning. 5g Net Of Carbs Or Less For A Healthy Lifestyle.

Marta Greene

Text Copyright ©

Legal & Disclaimer

Table of Contents

INTRODUCTION

Chaffle is a very versatile food that you can simply match with other food. There are also numerous ways to make it flavorful. Chaffle variations are indeed limitless!

Chaffle Toast. You can top it with corned tuna, cracked chicken, bacon, sausage… you name it! Feel free to play with the toppings.

Pancake-like. Serve it like pancakes by mixing sugar free syrup and keto butter. You can also garnish it with strawberries, blueberries, raspberries or blackberries.

Sandwiches, burger buns and pizza chaffle. Since chaffle is a bread substitute, you can make it into a sandwich or a burger bun. You can also create keto pizza chaffle. Simply spread 1 tablespoon of keto marinara sauce onto your chaffle and add shredded cheese and pepperoni on top. You can sprinkle veggie toppings too like olives, mushroom, onions, green bell pepper and all others you can think of.

Sweet or Savory. Adding a bit of keto-friendly flour makes your chaffle more bready. If you are in for a sweet treat, you can mix cinnamon, vanilla or cocoa powder with keto sweetener. But if you are into strong flavors you can add herbs and spices like finely chopped Jalapeño, pepper, or any seasoning of your preference.

Trying different types of cheese also gives it a distinct flavor. Tickle your palate by putting in pepper jack cheese, cottage cheese, gorgonzola, parmesan cheese, brie, provolone, and ricotta.

CHAPTER 1: OVERVIEW OF THE INGREDIENTS AND TOOLS

What Can You Serve with Chaffles?

Chaffle is a very versatile food that you can simply match with other food. There are also numerous ways to make it flavorful. Chaffle variations are indeed limitless!

Chaffle Toast. You can top it with corned tuna, cracked chicken, bacon, sausage... you name it! Feel free to play with the toppings.

Pancake-like. Serve it like pancakes by mixing sugar free syrup and keto butter. You can also garnish it with strawberries, blueberries, raspberries or blackberries.

Sandwiches, burger buns and pizza chaffle. Since chaffle is a bread substitute, you can make it into a sandwich or a burger bun. You can also create keto pizza chaffle. Simply spread 1 tablespoon of keto marinara sauce onto your chaffle and add shredded cheese and pepperoni on top. You can sprinkle veggie toppings too like olives, mushroom, onions, green bell pepper and all others you can think of.

Sweet or Savory. Adding a bit of keto-friendly flour makes your chaffle more bready. If you are in for a sweet treat, you can mix cinnamon, vanilla or cocoa powder with keto sweetener. But if you are into strong flavors you can add herbs and spices like finely chopped Jalapeño, pepper, or any seasoning of your preference.

Trying different types of cheese also gives it a distinct flavor. Tickle your palate by putting in pepper jack cheese, cottage cheese, gorgonzola, parmesan cheese, brie, provolone, and ricotta. There are so many cheeses to choose from!

Chaffle is making rounds on the internet as the latest keto recipe. It is an ideal and yummy substitute for bread. But whether you are on a ketogenic diet or just plain curious, making chaffle is easy.

Chaffle is basically a low carb waffle and you just need two main ingredients for it: egg and cheese. It also only takes a few minutes to cook in a mini waffle maker.

A newly coined term, chaffle is simply a combination of two words: cheese and waffle.

How to Make a Chaffle

Preparation is no-sweat!

First off, beat one egg in a mixing bowl until you achieve the desired consistency and add ½ cup of finely shredded mozzarella cheese. Preheat the mini waffle iron then pour the mixture into it. Cook until golden brown for about three to four minutes and presto, you already have your chaffle. Let it sit for a minute or two to make it crispy and just repeat the steps using the remaining batter.

If you find the taste too eggy, you can add a tablespoon of almond flour or any keto-friendly flour like coconut flour, psyllium husk flour, ground flax seed and the like. You can also top it with sugar free syrup and butter.

You can also try other kinds of cheese to see what will make your taste buds happier.

If you want it crunchier, you have to sprinkle shredded cheese on the waffle maker first and let it melt for half a minute before adding the mixture.

This is just the classic chaffle though. Remember that you can be creative with it and possibilities are endless!

Chaffles can be used for hamburger bun, hotdog bun, sandwich and pizza crust. You can also make it sweet or savory.

What Kind of Waffle Maker for Chaffles?

A mini waffle iron is perfect for making chaffles as it produces the ideal size (4 inches to be exact), cooks them fast and crisp them up.

If do not have one yet, choose the one that has a nonstick coating but chemical-free. The Dash mini waffle maker has recently been gaining popularity in the internet world.

If it is your first time to use this kind of appliance, don't worry because it's user-friendly and will definitely not eat much space in your cupboard.

But if you think using a mini waffle maker is time consuming because it makes 1 chaffle at a time, you can opt for a waffle maker that can make four chaffles at a time. This is ideal for a big family or for someone who would like to cook in batch in order to be able to store ready-made food on the fridge.

You can also use a Belgian waffle maker if you have this available at home. Since it is big, you need to adjust the recipe: 3 eggs are to 1.5 cup of cheese. You may also need to brush or spray oil onto the plate of this waffle maker so chaffle won't stick.

Gluten-Free Flour Alternatives

For those of you just starting out, gluten-free baking can sound incredibly daunting. As you are probably aware, gluten is the protein that is found in products including barley, wheat, and rye. If you read a food item with unbleached, refined flour, or wheat in the title, it probably contains gluten.

Luckily for all of us, there are many gluten-free flours that are readily available at our favorite stores. Many companies are hopping on the gluten-free bandwagon to help individuals who are gluten intolerant, gluten sensitive, and who are Celiac. For some, you may not even be able to tell the difference in your baked goods, which is good for those of us trying to cook for a family of picky eaters!

Almond Flour

You probably could have guessed this, but almond flour is made by grinding almonds into a coarse powder. Almond flour can be made using almonds without skin or blanched almonds. Almond flour is an excellent alternative as it is low in carbohydrates and high in fiber. If you are diabetic or trying to avoid carbohydrates in your diet, almond flour is an excellent choice. Almond flour is best used in recipes such as cookies and quick bread. If you are trying to make a cake with your bread machine, you will want to use finer almond flour.

Oat Flour

Oat Flour is another popular gluten-free alternative for flour. While oats themselves are gluten-free, you will need to be sure that they are not cross contaminated when they are blended. You will want to be especially careful if you have Celiac disease. If you are really crafty, oat flour is incredibly easy to make on your own! All you have to do is place the oats in a food processor and pulse until you achieve the desired texture. While these oats do have a mild taste, they typically have a dense texture. Oat flour is great for cookies, cakes, and pancakes! Oat flour also provides an excellent amount of protein and fiber. If you are looking to lower cholesterol and risk of heart disease, oat flour is an excellent choice for you.

Coconut Flour

Coconut products are becoming more and more popular on the market; it is no surprise that coconut flour is becoming more popular as well. Coconut flour is created from the inside meat of the coconut being dried and ground into a fine powder. This specific type of flour has healthy fats, high in protein, and low in carbohydrates. If you have a nut allergy, wheat allergy, or diabetes, coconut flour will be an excellent alternative for your baking needs. The one thing you should know before purchasing coconut flour is that it is typically sweet from the coconut. It also has a strong scent of coconut and typically has a finer texture compared to other flours. If you do not like coconut, this taste can be hard to mask. However, this flour is excellent for bread, brownies, and cinnamon buns.

Brown Rice Flour

Rice flour is by far one of the most popular flour alternatives to using in gluten-free baking. There are several different types including white rice flour, brown rice flour, and even sweet rice flour. The texture of these flours, while extremely fine is also kind of gritty. On top of this benefit, the rice flour is typically mild in taste and can be mixed into several baking products. This type of flour is best used in bread, brownies, pancakes, and cakes. Rice flour will typically be the cheapest alternative flour you will find on the market.

Gluten-Free Baking Mix

If you do not feel like messing around with all different flours, gluten-free baking flour will be perfect for you. This is a specific mixture if a combination of flours and grains that are created to mimic all-purpose flour. This type of baking mix can be used one for one, meaning that a recipe that requires one cup of all-purpose flour can use one cup of the gluten-free flour mix. The good news is that this baking mixed can be used in all different types of gluten-free baking but typically will cost you a bit more.

Sorghum Flour

If you are like me, you probably have not heard much about sorghum flour. This type of flour if a gluten-free grain that is soft in texture and sweet in flavor. There are many cereal grains that use sorghum flour. This grain is high in protein, fiber, and is an excellent source of antioxidants. Typically, this flour will be used in recipes for muffins, bread, and pizzas. Sorghum flour is also used in beer, but this is a book for baking, not beer!

Buckwheat Flour

While buckwheat is sometimes associated with gluten, buckwheat comes from a completely different botanical family from wheat. This type of flour is excellent for those with high blood pressure and type two diabetes. Buckwheat typically has a nutty flavor and is excellent for making bread. You will want to make sure the flour has not been exposed to nuts during manufacturing if you also have a nut allergy.

Quinoa Flour

If you are looking to make your bread and baked goods a bit healthier, quinoa flour will be an excellent choice. Generally, this type of flour is high in protein and is known to be the healthiest of all of the grains. If you are vegetarian or vegan, this flour can provide you with the amino acids you need in your diet. It can also help if you have high blood pressure or high blood sugar levels. Typically, quinoa flour has a nutty flavor that pairs well with waffles, pancakes, bread, and other baked goods.

Xanthan Gum

Before we move onto the fun part of baking, you must learn that xanthan gum is going to be your new best friend. You may not realize this, but many of the gluten-free flour alternatives lack a binding agent. A binding agent is helpful to hold your food together, much like gluten does when used in baking and cooking. The moment you remove gluten, all mixtures will typically crumble and fall apart. Xanthan gum is made from lactose, sucrose, and glucose that have been fermented from a specific bacterium. When this is added to liquid, it creates a gum and is used with gluten-free baking. As a general guide, you will be using one teaspoon of xanthan gum for one cup of gluten-free flour that you use. For some mixes, this gum is already added so when you are baking; you will always want to check the ingredient label. It should be noted that xanthan gum can be expensive, but it will last you a long time.

If you have an allergy to xanthan gum, you can find ways around it. Instead, you can try using psyllium husks, ground flaxseeds, or ground chia seeds. Psyllium can be sold in full husks or in powder. As you bake more, you will soon find what works for you, and what doesn't! For a quick reference of flours, you can use while baking gluten-free, refer to the list below.

Arrowroot Flour

Arrowroot flour and starch are excellent alternatives for cornstarch. Unlike corn, this plant is not genetically modified like cornstarch and acts as a thickening agent. If you are looking to make your cakes and bread softer, arrowroot flour will be the way to go. The great news is that arrowroot flour has no flavor and will not overwhelm the flavors of your bread. This flour is also excellent for puddings, soups, and sauces as well.

Bean Flours

Bean flours are another alternative that you can use. It is similar with arrowroot or cornstarch which can be used as a thickener. Available kinds of bean flours are the Soy Bean, Garbanzo, and the Fava Beans.

Nut Flours

Nut flours are derived from a variety of nuts which are raw and/or dried and have been ground to a fine powder. Nut flours bring texture and moisture due to the oils inherent in the nuts themselves and bring about a rich taste. Notable nut flour variants are – hazelnuts, coconut, chestnut, and the popular kind, the almond flours.

White Flours

This type of flour comes from White Rice, Tapioca, Sweet Rice, Potato, Cornstarch, and Arrowroot.

Whole Grain Flours

Whole grain flours come from Teff, Sweet Potato, Sorghum, Quinoa, Oats, Millet, Mesquite, Corn, Buckwheat, and Brown Rice

Before you begin baking, I want to remind you that more than likely, you are going to make mistakes! You cannot expect yourself to suddenly become a master-baker just because you picked up one book!

As mentioned earlier, you are probably used to baking one way and one way only. I invite you to return to a beginner's mindset. As you learn the new textures of your flours and doughs, expect to bake some ugly loaves of bread first. Eventually, you will get the hang of it and enjoy your delicious meals! When you think about it, the worst that can happen is a few bad, baked goods! I invite you to push past these failures and try again.

Whenever you make a mistake try to make a note what part of the recipe you had trouble with. Was it with the measurements? Was it with the time of baking? Or maybe how you prepared the dough? These things tend to be a little specific and it is pertinent that you would stick to the recipe at first, perfect it, and then try tweaking the recipe to fit your palate. Of course, I encourage you to put variations depending on your preference as what you enjoy may be different from what others enjoy. Start with the basics then move forward. Eventually, you will get the hang of it!

Baking basics

You'll need to have just a few pieces of equipment and learn some basic techniques before getting started in your baking practice.

BANNETON OR PROOFING BASKET: For the final proof, the dough needs to be placed in a basket that will allow air to circulate. You can buy baskets specifically for this called bannetons, which are made of cane. If you aren't ready to invest in a couple of bannetons just yet, a round or oval basket from a thrift store can be lined with a floured kitchen towel for a more affordable option. When I first started out, I had a ragtag collection of round and oval-shaped baskets, and they worked just fine.

BOWLS: I love using the large metal mixing bowl that I found at a restaurant supply store, but any bowl will do. Make sure you have a variety of sizes so you can measure out different quantities of ingredients. Whenever I shop at thrift stores, I like finding small bowls for a few cents here and there to add to my collection. Having little bowls for ingredients in smaller amounts, like salt, yeast, chopped herbs, and so on, is nice, but it's not absolutely necessary—any vessel will do.

CAST IRON DUTCH OVEN: This is needed for creating a high-heat, steam-enclosed environment to bake loaves in, and it's the best investment for baking artisan-style loaves in a home oven. You can find these on Amazon for about $35 or at your local kitchen store. Many people already have a cast iron or ceramic Dutch oven in their kitchen, but if you don't, it's well worth the investment. I use a Dutch oven in many of the recipes in the book.

DOUGH SCRAPER: I recommend getting a metal and a plastic dough scraper. They cost just a few dollars at kitchen stores, at restaurant supply stores, or on Amazon, and they are so useful. A metal scraper is helpful for cutting and scraping dough off your work area, and a plastic scraper is flexible enough to help scrape the dough out of the bowl after rising.

KITCHEN SCALE: Almost all of the ingredients in the recipes are measured in grams, so you will need a kitchen scale that weighs in metrics. Weighing your ingredients is the best way to get the most consistent results in your baking, and once you get used to weighing your ingredients, I promise you won't want to go back. It is so much simpler and makes a huge difference in the final loaf of bread. Kitchen scales are relatively inexpensive these days; small ones can be found for around $20. They typically have a "mode" button that will easily switch them from ounces to grams.

LOAF PANS: I recommend buying two 9-by-5-by-3-inch rectangular loaf pans, which is probably the most common size found at stores. My favorite pan is from USA Pan, and it can be found online. The loaves never ever stick to them. I use a 9-by-5-by-3-inch loaf pan for all of the loaf-style breads in this book.

NOTEBOOK AND PEN: I can't say enough that when you are starting out, different baking results will occur and you will want to know why you got those results. The only way to find out is to record what you did. Think of it like running a series of scientific experiments. Everything being equal, knowing what variables have changed and what haven't can lead you to where you went right or wrong.

PEEL: This is a flat wooden board with a handle for loading bread or pizza onto a baking stone in the oven. If you don't have one, it's no problem—I used a thin wooden cutting board for years, and it is a fine option.

PIZZA STONE OR BAKING STONE: These are preheated in the oven and help build the perfect crust while baking bread and pizza. If you don't have one, you can bake on an inverted baking sheet lined with parchment, but the results won't be quite the same.

RAZOR BLADE OR LAME: A razor blade is the best tool for slashing the top of a loaf of bread. A lame is a tool that holds the razor blade safely and has a nice handle, which makes it even easier to make precision slashes. My favorite lame is made by Mure & Peyrot and can be found on Amazon for only $15. You won't need one for the *first chapter* of this book, but you will as you move on to more advanced recipes.

RIMMED BAKING SHEET: This is an item you likely have in your kitchen already, and if not, it's a worthwhile investment. I usually use a 12-by-18-inch or a 16-by-24-inch baking sheet, which can be found at restaurant supply stores and online. In some recipes within this book, I call for a 16-by-24-inch baking sheet, but if a 12-by-18-inch sheet fits better in your oven, feel free to use that instead.

THERMOMETER: To achieve consistency in your baking, you'll need to know the temperature of your water and the ingredients. Buy a probe thermometer to check temperatures of ingredients. I also recommend you have an oven thermometer to be sure the temperature of your oven is accurate. You can purchase these for around $20 on Amazon and in most grocery stores.

Other items you may need that are usually part of any kitchen:

- Kitchen towels

- Nonstick cooking spray

- Parchment paper

- Pastry brush

- Plastic wrap

- Scissors

- Spray bottle

- Rubber spatula

CHAPTER 2: TIPS

- Preparation and cooking

Preheat. Make sure the waffle iron is hot enough before you pour in the batter. This is crucial in producing crunchy, golden brown chaffles. It will also make the mixture less likely to stick and therefore easier to clean up.

Put no oil. Chaffles are oil-free. To cook it just pour batter directly onto the waffle maker. No need to spray oil onto it.

Let it cool. Allowing chaffles to cool make it crispier.

Adjust the taste. You can use egg whites only to minimize the eggy taste. You can also add 1 tablespoon of low carb flour to make the texture more like that of the bread.

Adding 4 tablespoons of cream cheese also lessen eggy taste. Mixing a tablespoon of nutritional yeast also helps.

If you want your chaffles sweet, you can mix keto sweeteners like stevia in the batter. You can put extra flavor like vanilla or cinnamon. If you want it savory, you can mix garlic powder, onion powder and other herbs and spices.

For those who want their chaffles less cheesy, mixing mozzarella cheese is highly recommended but for a strong cheesy taste, use cheddar cheese instead.

Experiment with the recipe. You can eat it plain but you can also put toppings of your choice, make it into a pizza, burger, sandwich and even turn it into a taco shell.

Be patient. Do not open the waffle iron until after four minutes or when chaffle is not steaming anymore. That's a pretty good hint that its already done.

- Safety and Cleanliness

Avoid accident. Keep the cord out of reach by children of pets.

Set your timer. You don't want burnt chaffles. Do not leave your waffle maker while cooking lest you forget it and create a fire. To save time while waiting, prepare the other items or ingredients.

Don't Overfill. Avoid overfilling the waffle iron to avoid overflowing of mixture. You can use a squeeze bottle for a spic and span transfer of batter to waffle maker.

Avoid Mess. Put the waffle maker on a big plate or use a silicone mat so cleaning up would be a breeze in case of batter overflow.

Clean outright. Clean your waffle maker immediately to avoid hardening of batter. Use toothbrush to clean in between the teeth of the waffle iron and wipe it with paper towel with a few drops of vinegar.

Can You Make Chaffles Without a Waffle Maker?

No waffle maker? No problem! Because making chaffle without waffle iron is possible.

For one, you can use a grill pan. To prepare, just put the grill pan over medium heat.

When warm enough brush coconut oil onto it or any kind of cooking oil for keto diet.

Spoon the mixture onto the pan, lower the heat and cook it until you get the desired texture then flip. You can also use a pan for this; chaffle will taste the same but looks different.

How to Make Chaffles Crispy

Chaffle is well-loved for its crisp on the outside and fluffiness on the inside. But in order to achieve the crispiness that want you, let it cool first before serving or before adding other ingredients.

How to Store Chaffles

If you want to make large batch of chaffles for future consumption you can definitely store it in the refrigerator for as long as 3 to 5 days. Let your chaffles sit for some minutes until cool and put them in an airtight container before storing in the fridge. No worries because it will still be tasty after a few days.

Can You Freeze Chaffles?

Yes, you can!

If you are up for mass production, freezing chaffles is the way to go. You can put two chaffles in a small freezer bag, just don't forget to place parchment paper in between them so that they will not stick. Make sure to seal the freezer bag properly so the chaffle will not absorb the odor of other food stored in the freezer.

How to Reheat Chaffles

There are a lot of options for reheating chaffles: you can use air fryer, toaster oven, oven or toaster. Reheating with these appliances helps bring back the crisp. You can also microwave chaffles for about 1 to 2 minutes. Outcome isn't crunchy though.

CHAPTER 3: RECIPES

Beginners

01. Chocolate Melt Chaffles

Preparation Time: 15 minutes

Cooking Time: 36 minutes

Servings: 4

Ingredients

For the chaffles:

- 2 eggs, beaten
- ¼ cup finely grated Gruyere cheese
- 2 tbsp heavy cream
- 1 tbsp coconut flour
- 2 tbsp cream cheese, softened
- 3 tbsp unsweetened cocoa powder
- 2 tsp vanilla extract
- A pinch of salt

For the chocolate sauce:

- 1/3 cup + 1 tbsp heavy cream
- 1 ½ oz unsweetened baking chocolate, chopped
- 1 ½ tsp sugar-free maple syrup
- 1 ½ tsp vanilla extract

Directions:

For the chaffles:

1. Preheat the waffle iron.
2. In a medium bowl, mix all the ingredients for the chaffles.
3. Open the iron and add a quarter of the mixture. Close and cook until crispy, 7 minutes.
4. Transfer the chaffle to a plate and make 3 more with the remaining batter.

For the chocolate sauce:

1. Pour the heavy cream into saucepan and simmer over low heat, 3 minutes.
2. Turn the heat off and add the chocolate. Allow melting for a few minutes and stir until fully melted, 5 minutes.
3. Mix in the maple syrup and vanilla extract.
4. Assemble the chaffles in layers with the chocolate sauce sandwiched between each layer.
5. Slice and serve immediately.

Nutrition:

Calories 172

Fats 13.57g

Carbs 6.65g

Net Carbs 3.65g

Protein 5.76g

02. Chaffles with Keto Ice Cream

Preparation Time: 10 minutes

Cooking Time: 14 minutes

Servings: 2

Ingredients:

- 1 egg, beaten
- ½ cup finely grated mozzarella cheese
- ¼ cup almond flour
- 2 tbsp swerve confectioner's sugar
- 1/8 tsp xanthan gum
- Low-carb ice cream (flavor of your choice) for serving

Directions:

1. Preheat the waffle iron.
2. In a medium bowl, mix all the ingredients except the ice cream.
3. Open the iron and add half of the mixture. Close and cook until crispy, 7 minutes.
4. Transfer the chaffle to a plate and make second one with the remaining batter.
5. On each chaffle, add a scoop of low carb ice cream, fold into half-moons and enjoy.

Nutrition:

Calories 89

Fats 6.48g

Carbs 1.67g

Net Carbs 1.37g

Protein 5.91g

03. Strawberry Shortcake Chaffle Bowls

Preparation Time: 10 minutes

Cooking Time: 28 minutes

Servings: 4

Ingredients:

- 1 egg, beaten
- ½ cup finely grated mozzarella cheese
- 1 tbsp almond flour
- ¼ tsp baking powder
- 2 drops cake batter extract
- 1 cup cream cheese, softened
- 1 cup fresh strawberries, sliced
- 1 tbsp sugar-free maple syrup

Directions:

1. Preheat a waffle bowl maker and grease lightly with cooking spray.
2. Meanwhile, in a medium bowl, whisk all the ingredients except the cream cheese and strawberries.
3. Open the iron, pour in half of the mixture, cover, and cook until crispy, 6 to 7 minutes.
4. Remove the chaffle bowl onto a plate and set aside.
5. Make a second chaffle bowl with the remaining batter.
6. To serve, divide the cream cheese into the chaffle bowls and top with the strawberries.
7. Drizzle the filling with the maple syrup and serve.

Nutrition:

Calories 235

Fats 20.62g

Carbs 5.9g

Net Carbs 5g

Protein 7.51g

04. Chaffles with Raspberry Syrup

Preparation Time: 10 minutes

Cooking Time: 38 minutes

Servings: 4

Ingredients:

For the chaffles:

- 1 egg, beaten
- ½ cup finely shredded cheddar cheese
- 1 tsp almond flour
- 1 tsp vanilla extract
- 1 tsp sour cream

For the raspberry syrup:

- 1 cup fresh raspberries
- ¼ cup swerve sugar
- ¼ cup water

Directions:

For the chaffles:

1. Preheat the waffle iron.
2. Meanwhile, in a medium bowl, mix the egg, cheddar cheese, almond flour, and sour cream.
3. Open the iron, pour in half of the mixture, cover, and cook until crispy, 7 minutes.
4. Remove the chaffle onto a plate and make another with the remaining batter.

For the raspberry syrup:

1. Meanwhile, add the raspberries, swerve sugar, water, and vanilla extract to a medium pot. Set over low heat and cook until the raspberries soften and sugar becomes syrupy. Occasionally stir while mashing the raspberries as you go. Turn the heat off when your desired consistency is achieved and set aside to cool.
2. Drizzle some syrup on the chaffles and enjoy when ready.

Nutrition:

Calories 105

Fats 7.11g

Carbs 4.31g

Net Carbs 2.21g

Protein 5.83g

05. Chaffle Cannoli

Preparation Time: 15 minutes

Cooking Time: 28 minutes

Servings: 4

Ingredients:

For the chaffles:

- 1 large egg
- 1 egg yolk
- 3 tbsp butter, melted
- 1 tbso swerve confectioner's
- 1 cup finely grated Parmesan cheese
- 2 tbsp finely grated mozzarella cheese

For the cannoli filling:

- ½ cup ricotta cheese
- 2 tbsp swerve confectioner's sugar
- 1 tsp vanilla extract
- 2 tbsp unsweetened chocolate chips for garnishing

Directions:

1. Preheat the waffle iron.
2. Meanwhile, in a medium bowl, mix all the ingredients for the chaffles.
3. Open the iron, pour in a quarter of the mixture, cover, and cook until crispy, 7 minutes.
4. Remove the chaffle onto a plate and make 3 more with the remaining batter.
5. Meanwhile, for the cannoli filling:
6. Beat the ricotta cheese and swerve confectioner's sugar until smooth. Mix in the vanilla.
7. On each chaffle, spread some of the filling and wrap over.
8. Garnish the creamy ends with some chocolate chips.
9. Serve immediately.

Nutrition:

Calories 308

Fats 25.05g

Carbs 5.17g

Net Carbs 5.17g

Protein 15.18g

06. Blueberry Chaffles

Preparation Time: 10 minutes

Cooking Time: 28 minutes

Servings: 4

Ingredients:

- 1 egg, beaten
- ½ cup finely grated mozzarella cheese
- 1 tbsp cream cheese, softened
- 1 tbsp sugar-free maple syrup + extra for topping
- ½ cup blueberries
- ¼ tsp vanilla extract

Directions:

1. Preheat the waffle iron.
2. In a medium bowl, mix all the ingredients.
3. Open the iron, lightly grease with cooking spray and pour in a quarter of the mixture.
4. Close the iron and cook until golden brown and crispy, 7 minutes.
5. Remove the chaffle onto a plate and set aside.
6. Make the remaining chaffles with the remaining mixture.
7. Drizzle the chaffles with maple syrup and serve afterward.

Nutrition:

Calories 137

Fats 9.07g

Carbs 4.02g

Net Carbs 3.42g

Protein 9.59g

07. Nutter Butter Chaffles

Preparation Time: 15 minutes

Cooking Time: 14 minutes

Servings: 2

Ingredients:

For the chaffles:

- 2 tbsp sugar-free peanut butter powder
- 2 tbsp maple (sugar-free) syrup
- 1 egg, beaten
- ¼ cup finely grated mozzarella cheese
- ¼ tsp baking powder
- ¼ tsp almond butter
- ¼ tsp peanut butter extract
- 1 tbsp softened cream cheese

For the frosting:

- ½ cup almond flour
- 1 cup peanut butter
- 3 tbsp almond milk
- ½ tsp vanilla extract
- ½ cup maple (sugar-free) syrup

Directions:

1. Preheat the waffle iron.
2. Meanwhile, in a medium bowl, mix all the ingredients until smooth.
3. Open the iron and pour in half of the mixture.
4. Close the iron and cook until crispy, 6 to 7 minutes.
5. Remove the chaffle onto a plate and set aside.
6. Make a second chaffle with the remaining batter.
7. While the chaffles cool, make the frosting.
8. Pour the almond flour in a medium saucepan and stir-fry over medium heat until golden.
9. Transfer the almond flour to a blender and top with the remaining frosting ingredients. Process until smooth.
10. Spread the frosting on the chaffles and serve afterward.

Nutrition:

Calories 239

Fats 15.48g

Carbs 17.42g

Net Carbs 15.92g

Protein 7.52g

08. Chaffled Brownie Sundae

Preparation Time: 12 minutes

Cooking Time: 30 minutes

Servings: 4

Ingredients:

For the chaffles:

- 2 eggs, beaten
- 1 tbsp unsweetened cocoa powder
- 1 tbsp erythritol
- 1 cup finely grated mozzarella cheese

For the topping:

- 3 tbsp unsweetened chocolate, chopped
- 3 tbsp unsalted butter
- ½ cup swerve sugar
- Low-carb ice cream for topping
- 1 cup whipped cream for topping
- 3 tbsp sugar-free caramel sauce

Directions:

For the chaffles:

1. Preheat the waffle iron.
2. Meanwhile, in a medium bowl, mix all the ingredients for the chaffles.
3. Open the iron, pour in a quarter of the mixture, cover, and cook until crispy, 7 minutes.
4. Remove the chaffle onto a plate and make 3 more with the remaining batter.
5. Plate and set aside.

For the topping:

1. Meanwhile, melt the chocolate and butter in a medium saucepan with occasional stirring, 2 minutes.

To Servings:

1. Divide the chaffles into wedges and top with the ice cream, whipped cream, and swirl the chocolate sauce and caramel sauce on top.
2. Serve immediately.

Nutrition:

Calories 165   Fats 11.39g   Carbs 3.81g   Net Carbs 2.91g   Protein 12.79g

09. Brie and Blackberry Chaffles

Preparation Time: 15 minutes

Cooking Time: 36 minutes

Servings: 4

Ingredients:

For the chaffles:

- 2 eggs, beaten
- 1 cup finely grated mozzarella cheese
- For the topping:

- 1 ½ cups blackberries
- 1 lemon, 1 tsp zest and 2 tbsp juice
- 1 tbsp erythritol
- 4 slices Brie cheese

Directions:

For the chaffles:

1. Preheat the waffle iron.
2. Meanwhile, in a medium bowl, mix the eggs and mozzarella cheese.
3. Open the iron, pour in a quarter of the mixture, cover, and cook until crispy, 7 minutes.
4. Remove the chaffle onto a plate and make 3 more with the remaining batter.
5. Plate and set aside.

For the topping:

1. In a medium pot, add the blackberries, lemon zest, lemon juice, and erythritol. Cook until the blackberries break and the sauce thickens, 5 minutes. Turn the heat off.
2. Arrange the chaffles on the baking sheet and place two Brie cheese slices on each. Top with blackberry mixture and transfer the baking sheet to the oven.
3. Bake until the cheese melts, 2 to 3 minutes.
4. Remove from the oven, allow cooling and serve afterward.

Nutrition:

Calories 576

Fats 42.22g

Carbs 7.07g

Net Carbs 3.67g

Protein 42.35g

10. Carrot Chaffle Cake

Preparation Time: 15 minutes

Cooking Time: 24 minutes

Servings: 6

Ingredients:

- 1 egg, beaten
- 2 tablespoons melted butter
- ½ cup carrot, shredded
- ¾ cup almond flour
- 1 teaspoon baking powder
- 2 tablespoons heavy whipping cream
- 2 tablespoons sweetener
- 1 tablespoon walnuts, chopped
- 1 teaspoon pumpkin spice
- 2 teaspoons cinnamon

Directions:

1. Preheat your waffle maker.
2. In a large bowl, combine all the ingredients.
3. Pour some of the mixture into the waffle maker.
4. Close and cook for 4 minutes.
5. Repeat steps until all the remaining batter has been used.

Nutrition:

Calories 294

Total Fat 26.7g

Saturated Fat 12g

Cholesterol 133mg

Sodium 144mg

Potassium 421mg

Total Carbohydrate 11.6g

Dietary Fiber 4.5g

Protein 6.8g

Total Sugars 1.7g

11. Cereal Chaffle Cake

Preparation Time: 5 minutes

Cooking Time: 8 minutes

Servings: 2

Ingredients:

- 1 egg
- 2 tablespoons almond flour
- ½ teaspoon coconut flour
- 1 tablespoon melted butter
- 1 tablespoon cream cheese
- 1 tablespoon plain cereal, crushed
- ¼ teaspoon vanilla extract
- ¼ teaspoon baking powder
- 1 tablespoon sweetener
- 1/8 teaspoon xanthan gum

Directions:

1. Plug in your waffle maker to preheat.
2. Add all the ingredients in a large bowl.
3. Mix until well blended.
4. Let the batter rest for 2 minutes before cooking.
5. Pour half of the mixture into the waffle maker.
6. Seal and cook for 4 minutes.
7. Make the next chaffle using the same steps.

Nutrition:

Calories154

Total Fat 21.2g

Saturated Fat 10 g

Cholesterol 113.3mg

Sodium 96.9mg

Potassium 453 mg

Total Carbohydrate 5.9g

Dietary Fiber 1.7g

Protein 4.6g

Total Sugars 2.7g

12. Ham, Cheese & Tomato Chaffle Sandwich

Preparation Time: 5 minutes

Cooking Time: 10 minutes

Servings: 2

Ingredients:

- 1 teaspoon olive oil
- 2 slices ham
- 4 basic chaffles
- 1 tablespoon mayonnaise
- 2 slices Provolone cheese
- 1 tomato, sliced

Directions:

1. Add the olive oil to a pan over medium heat.
2. Cook the ham for 1 minute per side.
3. Spread the chaffles with mayonnaise.
4. Top with the ham, cheese and tomatoes.
5. Top with another chaffle to make a sandwich.

Nutrition:

Calories 198

Total Fat 14.7g

Saturated Fat 6.3g

Cholesterol 37mg

Sodium 664mg

Total Carbohydrate 4.6g

Dietary Fiber 0.7g

Total Sugars 1.5g

Protein 12.2g

Potassium 193mg

13. Broccoli & Cheese Chaffle

Preparation Time: 5 minutes

Cooking Time: 8 minutes

Servings: 2

Ingredients:

- ¼ cup broccoli florets
- 1 egg, beaten
- 1 tablespoon almond flour
- ¼ teaspoon garlic powder
- ½ cup cheddar cheese

Directions:

1. Preheat your waffle maker.
2. Add the broccoli to the food processor.
3. Pulse until chopped.
4. Add to a bowl.
5. Stir in the egg and the rest of the ingredients.
6. Mix well.
7. Pour half of the batter to the waffle maker.
8. Cover and cook for 4 minutes.
9. Repeat procedure to make the next chaffle.

Nutrition:

Calories 170

Total Fat 13 g

Saturated Fat 7 g

Cholesterol 112 mg

Sodium 211 mg

Potassium 94 mg

Total Carbohydrate 2 g

Dietary Fiber 1 g

Protein 11 g

Total Sugars 1 g

14. Chaffle with Sausage Gravy

Preparation Time: 5 minutes

Cooking Time: 15 minutes

Servings: 2

Ingredients:

- ¼ cup sausage, cooked
- 3 tablespoons chicken broth
- 2 teaspoons cream cheese
- 2 tablespoons heavy whipping cream
- ¼ teaspoon garlic powder
- Pepper to taste
- 2 basic chaffles

Directions:

1. Add the sausage, broth, cream cheese, cream, garlic powder and pepper to a pan over medium heat.
2. Bring to a boil and then reduce heat.
3. Simmer for 10 minutes or until the sauce has thickened.
4. Pour the gravy on top of the basic chaffles
5. Serve.

Nutrition:

Calories 212

Total Fat 17 g

Saturated Fat 10 g

Cholesterol 134 mg

Sodium 350 mg

Potassium 133 mg

Total Carbohydrate 3 g

Dietary Fiber 1 g

Protein 11 g

Total Sugars 1 g

15. Barbecue Chaffle

Preparation Time: 5 minutes

Cooking Time: 8 minutes

Servings: 2

Ingredients:

- 1 egg, beaten
- ½ cup cheddar cheese, shredded
- ½ teaspoon barbecue sauce
- ¼ teaspoon baking powder

Directions:

1. Plug in your waffle maker to preheat.
2. Mix all the ingredients in a bowl.
3. Pour half of the mixture to your waffle maker.
4. Cover and cook for 4 minutes.
5. Repeat the same steps for the next barbecue chaffle.

Nutrition:

Calories 295

Total Fat 23 g

Saturated Fat 13 g

Cholesterol 223 mg

Sodium 414 mg

Potassium 179 mg

Total Carbohydrate 2 g

Dietary Fiber 1 g

Protein 20 g

Total Sugars 1 g

16. Bacon & Chicken Ranch Chaffle

Preparation Time: 5 minutes

Cooking Time: 8 minutes

Servings: 2

Ingredients:

- 1 egg
- ¼ cup chicken cubes, cooked
- 1 slice bacon, cooked and chopped
- ¼ cup cheddar cheese, shredded
- 1 teaspoon ranch dressing powder

Directions:

1. Preheat your waffle maker.
2. In a bowl, mix all the ingredients.
3. Add half of the mixture to your waffle maker.
4. Cover and cook for 4 minutes.
5. Make the second chaffle using the same steps.

Nutrition:

Calories 200

Total Fat 14 g

Saturated Fat 6 g

Cholesterol 129 mg

Sodium 463 mg

Potassium 130 mg

Total Carbohydrate 2 g

Dietary Fiber 1 g

Protein 16 g

Total Sugars 1 g

17. Pumpkin & Pecan Chaffle

Preparation Time: 5 minutes

Cooking Time: 10 minutes

Servings: 2

Ingredients:

- 1 egg, beaten
- ½ cup mozzarella cheese, grated
- ½ teaspoon pumpkin spice
- 1 tablespoon pureed pumpkin
- 2 tablespoons almond flour
- 1 teaspoon sweetener
- 2 tablespoons pecans, chopped

Directions:

1. Turn on the waffle maker.
2. Beat the egg in a bowl.
3. Stir in the rest of the ingredients.
4. Pour half of the mixture into the device.
5. Seal the lid.
6. Cook for 5 minutes.
7. Remove the chaffle carefully.
8. Repeat the steps to make the second chaffle.

Nutrition:

Calories 210

Total Fat 17 g

Saturated Fat 10 g

Cholesterol 110 mg

Sodium 250 mg

Potassium 570 mg

Total Carbohydrate 4.6 g

Dietary Fiber 1.7 g

Protein 11 g

Total Sugars 2 g

18. Cheeseburger Chaffle

Preparation Time: 15 minutes

Cooking Time: 15 minutes

Servings: 2

Ingredients:

- 1 lb. ground beef
- 1 onion, minced

- 1 tsp. parsley, chopped
- 1 egg, beaten
- Salt and pepper to taste
- 1 tablespoon olive oil
- 4 basic chaffles
- 2 lettuce leaves
- 2 cheese slices
- 1 tablespoon dill pickles
- Ketchup
- Mayonnaise

Directions:

1. In a large bowl, combine the ground beef, onion, parsley, egg, salt and pepper.
2. Mix well.
3. Form 2 thick patties.
4. Add olive oil to the pan.
5. Place the pan over medium heat.
6. Cook the patty for 3 to 5 minutes per side or until fully cooked.
7. Place the patty on top of each chaffle.
8. Top with lettuce, cheese and pickles.
9. Squirt ketchup and mayo over the patty and veggies.
10. Top with another chaffle.

Nutrition:

Calories 325

Total Fat 16.3g

Saturated Fat 6.5g

Cholesterol 157mg

Sodium 208mg

Total Carbohydrate 3g

Dietary Fiber 0.7g

Total Sugars 1.4g

Protein 39.6g

Potassium 532mg

19. Double Choco Chaffle

Preparation Time: 5 minutes

Cooking Time: 10 minutes

Servings: 2

Ingredients:

- 1 egg

- 2 teaspoons coconut flour
- 2 tablespoons sweetener
- 1 tablespoon cocoa powder
- ¼ teaspoon baking powder
- 1 oz. cream cheese
- ½ teaspoon vanilla
- 1 tablespoon sugar-free chocolate chips

Directions:

1. Put all the ingredients in a large bowl.
2. Mix well.
3. Pour half of the mixture into the waffle maker.
4. Seal the device.
5. Cook for 4 minutes.
6. Uncover and transfer to a plate to cool.
7. Repeat the procedure to make the second chaffle.

Nutrition:

Calories 171

Total Fat 10.7g

Saturated Fat 5.3g

Cholesterol 97mg

Sodium 106mg

Potassium 179mg

Total Carbohydrate 3g

Dietary Fiber 4.8g

Protein 5.8g

Total Sugars 0.4g

20. Cream Cheese Chaffle

Preparation Time: 5 minutes

Cooking Time: 8 minutes

Servings: 2

Ingredients:

- 1 egg, beaten
- 1 oz. cream cheese

- ½ teaspoon vanilla
- 4 teaspoons sweetener
- ¼ teaspoon baking powder
- Cream cheese

Directions:

1. Preheat your waffle maker.
2. Add all the ingredients in a bowl.
3. Mix well.
4. Pour half of the batter into the waffle maker.
5. Seal the device.
6. Cook for 4 minutes.
7. Remove the chaffle from the waffle maker.
8. Make the second one using the same steps.
9. Spread remaining cream cheese on top before serving.

Nutrition:

Calories 169

Potassium 222mg

Total Fat 14.3g

Total Carbohydrate 4g

Saturated Fat 7.6g

Dietary Fiber 4g

Cholesterol 195mg

Protein 7.7g

Sodium 147mg

Total Sugars 0.7g

21. Creamy Chicken Chaffle Sandwich

Preparation Time: 5 minutes

Cooking Time: 10 minutes

Servings: 2

Ingredients:

- Cooking spray
- 1 cup chicken breast fillet, cubed
- Salt and pepper to taste

- ¼ cup all-purpose cream
- 4 garlic chaffles
- Parsley, chopped

Directions:

1. Spray your pan with oil.
2. Put it over medium heat.
3. Add the chicken fillet cubes.
4. Season with salt and pepper.
5. Reduce heat and add the cream.
6. Spread chicken mixture on top of the chaffle.
7. Garnish with parsley and top with another chaffle.

Nutrition:

Calories 273

Total Fat 38.4g

Saturated Fat 4.1g

Cholesterol 62mg

Sodium 373mg

Total Carbohydrate 22.5g

Dietary Fiber 1.1g

Total Sugars 3.2g

Protein 17.5g

Potassium 177mg

22. Turkey Chaffle Burger

Preparation Time: 10 minutes

Cooking Time: 10 minutes

Servings: 2

Ingredients:

- 2 cups ground turkey
- Salt and pepper to taste
- 1 tablespoon olive oil
- 4 garlic chaffles

- 1 cup Romaine lettuce, chopped
- 1 tomato, sliced
- Mayonnaise
- Ketchup

Directions:

1. Combine ground turkey, salt and pepper.
2. Form 2 thick burger patties.
3. Add the olive oil to a pan over medium heat.
4. Cook the turkey burger until fully cooked on both sides.
5. Spread mayo on the chaffle.
6. Top with the turkey burger, lettuce and tomato.
7. Squirt ketchup on top before topping with another chaffle.

Nutrition:

Calories 555

Total Fat 21.5g

Saturated Fat 3.5g

Cholesterol 117mg

Sodium 654mg

Total Carbohydrate 4.1g

Dietary Fiber 2.5g

Protein 31.7g

Total Sugars 1g

23. Savory Beef Chaffle

Preparation Time: 10 minutes

Cooking Time: 15 minutes

Servings: 2

Ingredients:

- 1 teaspoon olive oil
- 2 cups ground beef
- Garlic salt to taste
- 1 red bell pepper, sliced into strips
- 1 green bell pepper, sliced into strips
- 1 onion, minced
- 1 bay leaf
- 2 garlic chaffles

- Butter

Directions:

1. Put your pan over medium heat.
2. Add the olive oil and cook ground beef until brown.
3. Season with garlic salt and add bay leaf.
4. Drain the fat, transfer to a plate and set aside.
5. Discard the bay leaf.
6. In the same pan, cook the onion and bell peppers for 2 minutes.
7. Put the beef back to the pan.
8. Heat for 1 minute.
9. Spread butter on top of the chaffle.
10. Add the ground beef and veggies.
11. Roll or fold the chaffle.

Nutrition:

Calories 220

Total Fat 17.8g

Saturated Fat 8g

Cholesterol 76mg

Sodium 60mg

Total Carbohydrate 3g

Dietary Fiber 2g

Total Sugars 5.4g

Protein 27.1g

Potassium 537mg

24. Egg & Chives Chaffle Sandwich Roll

Preparation Time: 5 minutes

Cooking Time: 0 minute

Servings: 2

Ingredients:

- 2 tablespoons mayonnaise
- 1 hard-boiled egg, chopped
- 1 tablespoon chives, chopped
- 2 basic chaffles

Directions:

1. In a bowl, mix the mayo, egg and chives.
2. Spread the mixture on top of the chaffles.
3. Roll the chaffle.

Nutrition:

Calories 258

Total Fat 14.2g

Saturated Fat 2.8g

Cholesterol 171mg

Sodium 271mg

Potassium 71mg

Total Carbohydrate 7.5g

Dietary Fiber 0.1g

Protein 5.9g

Total Sugars 2.3g

25. Chocolate & Almond Chaffle

Preparation Time: 5 minutes

Cooking Time: 12 minutes

Servings: 3

Ingredients:

- 1 egg
- ¼ cup mozzarella cheese, shredded
- 1 oz. cream cheese
- 2 teaspoons sweetener
- 1 teaspoon vanilla

- 2 tablespoons cocoa powder
- 1 teaspoon baking powder
- 2 tablespoons almonds, chopped
- 4 tablespoons almond flour

Method:

1. Blend all the ingredients in a bowl while the waffle maker is preheating.
2. Pour some of the mixture into the waffle maker.
3. Close and cook for 4 minutes.
4. Transfer the chaffle to a plate. Let cool for 2 minutes.
5. Repeat steps using the remaining mixture.

Nutritional Value:

- Calories 167
- Total Fat 13.1g
- Saturated Fat 5g
- Cholesterol 99mg
- Sodium 99mg
- Potassium 481mg
- Total Carbohydrate 9.1g
- Dietary Fiber 3.8g
- Protein 7.8g
- Total Sugars 0.8g

26. Bruschetta Chaffle

Preparation Time: 5 minutes

Cooking Time: 5 minutes

Servings: 2

Ingredients:

- 2 basic chaffles
- 2 tablespoons sugar-free marinara sauce
- 2 tablespoons mozzarella, shredded
- 1 tablespoon olives, sliced

- 1 tomato sliced
- 1 tablespoon keto friendly pesto sauce
- Basil leaves

Directions:

1. Spread marinara sauce on each chaffle.
2. Spoon pesto and spread on top of the marinara sauce.
3. Top with the tomato, olives and mozzarella.
4. Bake in the oven for 3 minutes or until the cheese has melted.
5. Garnish with basil.
6. Serve and enjoy.

Nutrition:

Calories 182

Total Fat 11g

Saturated Fat 6.1g

Cholesterol 30mg

Sodium 508mg

Potassium 1mg

Total Carbohydrate 3.1g

Dietary Fiber 1.1g

Protein 16.8g

Total Sugars 1g

27. Asian Cauliflower Chaffles

Preparation Time: 20 minutes

Cooking Time: 28 minutes

Servings: 4

Ingredients:

For the chaffles:

- 1 cup cauliflower rice, steamed
- 1 large egg, beaten
- Salt and freshly ground black pepper to taste
- 1 cup finely grated Parmesan cheese
- 1 tsp sesame seeds
- ¼ cup chopped fresh scallions

For the dipping sauce:

- 3 tbsp coconut aminos
- 1 ½ tbsp plain vinegar
- 1 tsp fresh ginger puree
- 1 tsp fresh garlic paste
- 3 tbsp sesame oil
- 1 tsp fish sauce
- 1 tsp red chili flakes

Directions:

1. Preheat the waffle iron.
2. In a medium bowl, mix the cauliflower rice, egg, salt, black pepper, and Parmesan cheese.
3. Open the iron and add a quarter of the mixture. Close and cook until crispy, 7 minutes.
4. Transfer the chaffle to a plate and make 3 more chaffles in the same manner.
5. Meanwhile, make the dipping sauce.
6. In a medium bowl, mix all the ingredients for the dipping sauce.
7. Plate the chaffles, garnish with the sesame seeds and scallions and serve with the dipping sauce.

Nutrition:

Calories 231

Fats 18.88g

Carbs 6.32g

Net Carbs 5.42g

Protein 9.66g

28. Hot Dog Chaffles

Preparation Time: 15 minutes

Cooking Time: 14 minutes

Servings: 2

Ingredients:

- 1 egg, beaten
- 1 cup finely grated cheddar cheese
- 2 hot dog sausages, cooked
- Mustard dressing for topping
- 8 pickle slices

Directions:

1. Preheat the waffle iron.
2. In a medium bowl, mix the egg and cheddar cheese.
3. Open the iron and add half of the mixture. Close and cook until crispy, 7 minutes.
4. Transfer the chaffle to a plate and make a second chaffle in the same manner.
5. To serve, top each chaffle with a sausage, swirl the mustard dressing on top, and then divide the pickle slices on top.
6. Enjoy!

Nutrition:

Calories 231

Fats 18.29g

Carbs 2.8g

Net Carbs 2.6g

Protein 13.39g

29. Spicy Shrimp and Chaffles

Preparation Time: 15 minutes

Cooking Time: 31 minutes

Servings: 4

Ingredients:

For the shrimp:

- 1 tbsp olive oil
- 1 lb jumbo shrimp, peeled and deveined
- 1 tbsp Creole seasoning
- Salt to taste
- 2 tbsp hot sauce

- 3 tbsp butter
- 2 tbsp chopped fresh scallions to garnish

For the chaffles:

- 2 eggs, beaten
- 1 cup finely grated Monterey Jack cheese

Directions:

For the shrimp:

1. Heat the olive oil in a medium skillet over medium heat.
2. Season the shrimp with the Creole seasoning and salt. Cook in the oil until pink and opaque on both sides, 2 minutes.
3. Pour in the hot sauce and butter. Mix well until the shrimp is adequately coated in the sauce, 1 minute.
4. Turn the heat off and set aside.

For the chaffles:

1. Preheat the waffle iron.
2. In a medium bowl, mix the eggs and Monterey Jack cheese.
3. Open the iron and add a quarter of the mixture. Close and cook until crispy, 7 minutes.
4. Transfer the chaffle to a plate and make 3 more chaffles in the same manner.
5. Cut the chaffles into quarters and place on a plate.
6. Top with the shrimp and garnish with the scallions.
7. Serve warm.

Nutrition:

Calories 342

Fats 19.75g

Carbs 2.8g

Net Carbs 2.3g

Protein 36.01g

30. Chicken Jalapeño Chaffles

Preparation Time: 15 minutes

Cooking Time: 14 minutes

Servings: 2

Ingredients:

- 1/8 cup finely grated Parmesan cheese
- ¼ cup finely grated cheddar cheese
- 1 egg, beaten
- ½ cup cooked chicken breasts, diced
- 1 small jalapeño pepper, deseeded and minced
- 1/8 tsp garlic powder
- 1/8 tsp onion powder
- 1 tsp cream cheese, softened

Directions:

1. Preheat the waffle iron.
2. In a medium bowl, mix all the ingredients until adequately combined.
3. Open the iron and add half of the mixture. Close and cook until crispy, 7 minutes.
4. Transfer the chaffle to a plate and make a second chaffle in the same manner.
5. Allow cooling and serve afterward.

Nutrition:

Calories 201

Fats 11.49g

Carbs 3.76g

Net Carbs 3.36g

Protein 20.11g

31. Chicken and Chaffle Nachos

Preparation Time: 15 minutes

Cooking Time: 33 minutes

Servings: 4

Ingredients:

For the chaffles:

- 2 eggs, beaten
- 1 cup finely grated Mexican cheese blend

For the chicken-cheese topping:

- 2 tbsp butter
- 1 tbsp almond flour
- ¼ cup unsweetened almond milk
- 1 cup finely grated cheddar cheese + more to garnish
- 3 bacon slices, cooked and chopped

- 2 cups cooked and diced chicken breasts
- 2 tbsp hot sauce
- 2 tbsp chopped fresh scallions

Directions:

For the chaffles:

1. Preheat the waffle iron.
2. In a medium bowl, mix the eggs and Mexican cheese blend.
3. Open the iron and add a quarter of the mixture. Close and cook until crispy, 7 minutes.
4. Transfer the chaffle to a plate and make 3 more chaffles in the same manner.
5. Place the chaffles on serving plates and set aside for serving.

For the chicken-cheese topping:

1. Melt the butter in a large skillet and mix in the almond flour until brown, 1 minute.
2. Pour the almond milk and whisk until well combined. Simmer until thickened, 2 minutes.
3. Stir in the cheese to melt, 2 minutes and then mix in the bacon, chicken, and hot sauce.
4. Spoon the mixture onto the chaffles and top with some more cheddar cheese.
5. Garnish with the scallions and serve immediately.

Nutrition:

Calories 524

Fats 37.51g

Carbs 3.55g

Net Carbs 3.25g

Protein 41.86g

32. Buffalo Hummus Beef Chaffles

Preparation Time: 15 minutes

Cooking Time: 32 minutes

Servings: 4

Ingredients:

- 2 eggs
- 1 cup + ¼ cup finely grated cheddar cheese, divided
- 2 chopped fresh scallions
- Salt and freshly ground black pepper to taste
- 2 chicken breasts, cooked and diced
- ¼ cup buffalo sauce
- 3 tbsp low-carb hummus
- 2 celery stalks, chopped
- ¼ cup crumbled blue cheese for topping

Directions:

1. Preheat the waffle iron.
2. In a medium bowl, mix the eggs, 1 cup of the cheddar cheese, scallions, salt, and black pepper,

3. Open the iron and add a quarter of the mixture. Close and cook until crispy, 7 minutes.
4. Transfer the chaffle to a plate and make 3 more chaffles in the same manner.
5. Preheat the oven to 400 F and line a baking sheet with parchment paper. Set aside.
6. Cut the chaffles into quarters and arrange on the baking sheet.
7. In a medium bowl, mix the chicken with the buffalo sauce, hummus, and celery.
8. Spoon the chicken mixture onto each quarter of chaffles and top with the remaining cheddar cheese.
9. Place the baking sheet in the oven and bake until the cheese melts, 4 minutes.
10. Remove from the oven and top with the blue cheese.
11. Serve afterward.

Nutrition:

Calories 552	Carbs 6.97g	Protein 59.8g
Fats 28.37g	Net Carbs 6.07g	

33. Pulled Pork Chaffle Sandwiches

Preparation Time: 20 minutes

Cooking Time: 28 minutes

Servings: 4

Ingredients:

- 2 eggs, beaten
- 1 cup finely grated cheddar cheese
- ¼ tsp baking powder
- 2 cups cooked and shredded pork
- 1 tbsp sugar-free BBQ sauce
- 2 cups shredded coleslaw mix
- 2 tbsp apple cider vinegar
- ½ tsp salt
- ¼ cup ranch dressing

Directions:

1. Preheat the waffle iron.
2. In a medium bowl, mix the eggs, cheddar cheese, and baking powder.
3. Open the iron and add a quarter of the mixture. Close and cook until crispy, 7 minutes.

4. Transfer the chaffle to a plate and make 3 more chaffles in the same manner.
5. Meanwhile, in another medium bowl, mix the pulled pork with the BBQ sauce until well combined. Set aside.
6. Also, mix the coleslaw mix, apple cider vinegar, salt, and ranch dressing in another medium bowl.
7. When the chaffles are ready, on two pieces, divide the pork and then top with the ranch coleslaw. Cover with the remaining chaffles and insert mini skewers to secure the sandwiches.
8. Enjoy afterward.

Nutrition:

Calories 374

Net Carbs 8.2g

Fats 23.61g

Protein 28.05g

Carbs 8.2g

34. Okonomiyaki Chaffles

Preparation Time: 20 minutes

Cooking Time: 28 minutes

Servings: 4

Ingredients:

For the chaffles:

- 2 eggs, beaten
- 1 cup finely grated mozzarella cheese
- ½ tsp baking powder
- ¼ cup shredded radishes

For the sauce:

- 2 tsp coconut aminos
- 2 tbsp sugar-free ketchup
- 1 tbsp sugar-free maple syrup
- 2 tsp Worcestershire sauce

For the topping:

- 1 tbsp mayonnaise
- 2 tbsp chopped fresh scallions
- 2 tbsp bonito flakes
- 1 tsp dried seaweed powder
- 1 tbsp pickled ginger

Directions:

For the chaffles:

1. Preheat the waffle iron.
2. In a medium bowl, mix the eggs, mozzarella cheese, baking powder, and radishes.
3. Open the iron and add a quarter of the mixture. Close and cook until crispy, 7 minutes.
4. Transfer the chaffle to a plate and make a 3 more chaffles in the same manner.
5. For the sauce:
6. Combine the coconut aminos, ketchup, maple syrup, and Worcestershire sauce in a medium bowl and mix well.

For the topping:

1. In another mixing bowl, mix the mayonnaise, scallions, bonito flakes, seaweed powder, and ginger
2. To Servings:
3. Arrange the chaffles on four different plates and swirl the sauce on top. Spread the topping on the chaffles and serve afterward.

Nutrition:

Calories 90

Fats 3.32g

Carbs 2.97g

Net Carbs 2.17g

Protein 12.09g

35. Keto Reuben Chaffles

Preparation Time: 15 minutes

Cooking Time: 28 minutes

Servings: 4

Ingredients:

For the chaffles:

- 2 eggs, beaten
- 1 cup finely grated Swiss cheese
- 2 tsp caraway seeds
- 1/8 tsp salt
- ½ tsp baking powder

For the sauce:

- 2 tbsp sugar-free ketchup
- 3 tbsp mayonnaise
- 1 tbsp dill relish
- 1 tsp hot sauce

For the filling:

- 6 oz pastrami
- 2 Swiss cheese slices
- ¼ cup pickled radishes

Directions:

For the chaffles:

1. Preheat the waffle iron.
2. In a medium bowl, mix the eggs, Swiss cheese, caraway seeds, salt, and baking powder.
3. Open the iron and add a quarter of the mixture. Close and cook until crispy, 7 minutes.
4. Transfer the chaffle to a plate and make 3 more chaffles in the same manner.

For the sauce:

1. In another bowl, mix the ketchup, mayonnaise, dill relish, and hot sauce.
2. To assemble:
3. Divide on two chaffles; the sauce, the pastrami, Swiss cheese slices, and pickled radishes.
4. Cover with the other chaffles, divide the sandwich in halves and serve.

Nutrition:

Calories 316

Fats 21.78g

Carbs 6.52g

Net Carbs 5.42g

Protein 23.56g

36. Pumpkin-Cinnamon Churro Sticks

Preparation Time: 10 minutes

Cooking Time: 14 minutes

Servings: 2

Ingredients:

- 3 tbsp coconut flour
- ¼ cup pumpkin puree
- 1 egg, beaten
- ½ cup finely grated mozzarella cheese
- 2 tbsp sugar-free maple syrup + more for serving
- 1 tsp baking powder
- 1 tsp vanilla extract
- ½ tsp pumpkin spice seasoning
- 1/8 tsp salt
- 1 tbsp cinnamon powder

Directions:

1. Preheat the waffle iron.
2. Mix all the ingredients in a medium bowl until well combined.

3. Open the iron and add half of the mixture. Close and cook until golden brown and crispy, 7 minutes.
4. Remove the chaffle onto a plate and make 1 more with the remaining batter.
5. Cut each chaffle into sticks, drizzle the top with more maple syrup and serve after.

Nutrition Facts per Serving:

Calories 219

Fats 9.72g

Carbs 8.64g

Net Carbs 4.34g

Protein 25.27g

37. Keto Chocolate Fudge Chaffle

Preparation Time: 10 minutes

Cooking Time: 14 minutes

Servings: 2

Ingredients:

- 1 egg, beaten
- ¼ cup finely grated Gruyere cheese
- 2 tbsp unsweetened cocoa powder
- ¼ tsp baking powder
- ¼ tsp vanilla extract
- 2 tbsp erythritol
- 1 tsp almond flour
- 1 tsp heavy whipping cream
- A pinch of salt

Directions:

1. Preheat the waffle iron.
2. Add all the ingredients to a medium bowl and mix well.

3. Open the iron and add half of the mixture. Close and cook until golden brown and crispy, 7 minutes.
4. Remove the chaffle onto a plate and make another with the remaining batter.
5. Cut each chaffle into wedges and serve after.

Nutrition Facts per Serving:

Calories 173

Fats 13.08g

Carbs 3.98g

Net Carbs 2.28g

Protein 12.27g

38. Guacamole Chaffle Bites

Preparation Time: 10 minutes

Cooking Time: 14 minutes

Servings: 2

Ingredients:

- 1 large turnip, cooked and mashed
- 2 bacon slices, cooked and finely chopped
- ½ cup finely grated Monterey Jack cheese
- 1 egg, beaten
- 1 cup guacamole for topping

Directions:

1. Preheat the waffle iron.
2. Mix all the ingredients except for the guacamole in a medium bowl.
3. Open the iron and add half of the mixture. Close and cook for 4 minutes. Open the lid, flip the chaffle and cook further until golden brown and crispy, 3 minutes.
4. Remove the chaffle onto a plate and make another in the same manner.
5. Cut each chaffle into wedges, top with the guacamole and serve afterward.

Nutrition Facts per Serving:

Calories 311

Fats 22.52g

Carbs 8.29g

Net Carbs 5.79g

Protein 13.62g

39. Zucchini Parmesan Chaffles

Preparation Time: 10 minutes

Cooking Time: 14 minutes

Servings: 2

Ingredients:

- 1 cup shredded zucchini
- 1 egg, beaten
- ½ cup finely grated Parmesan cheese
- Salt and freshly ground black pepper to taste

Directions:

1. Preheat the waffle iron.
2. Put all the ingredients in a medium bowl and mix well.
3. Open the iron and add half of the mixture. Close and cook until crispy, 7 minutes.
4. Remove the chaffle onto a plate and make another with the remaining mixture.
5. Cut each chaffle into wedges and serve afterward.

Nutrition Facts per Serving:

Calories 138

Fats 9.07g

Carbs 3.81g

Net Carbs 3.71g

Protein 10.02g

40. Blue Cheese Chaffle Bites

Preparation Time: 10 minutes

Cooking Time: 14 minutes

Servings: 2

Ingredients:

- 1 egg, beaten
- ½ cup finely grated Parmesan cheese
- ¼ cup crumbled blue cheese
- 1 tsp erythritol

Directions:

1. Preheat the waffle iron.
2. Mix all the ingredients in a bowl.
3. Open the iron and add half of the mixture. Close and cook until crispy, 7 minutes.
4. Remove the chaffle onto a plate and make another with the remaining mixture.
5. Cut each chaffle into wedges and serve afterward.

Nutrition Facts per Serving:

Calories 196

Fats 13.91g

Carbs 4.03g

Net Carbs 4.03g

Protein 13.48g

Intermediate

41. Chaffle Fruit Snacks

Preparation Time: 10 minutes

Cooking Time: 14 minutes

Servings: 2

Ingredients:

- 1 egg, beaten
- ½ cup finely grated cheddar cheese
- ½ cup Greek yogurt for topping
- 8 raspberries and blackberries for topping

Directions:

1. Preheat the waffle iron.
2. Mix the egg and cheddar cheese in a medium bowl.
3. Open the iron and add half of the mixture. Close and cook until crispy, 7 minutes.
4. Remove the chaffle onto a plate and make another with the remaining mixture.
5. Cut each chaffle into wedges and arrange on a plate.
6. Top each waffle with a tablespoon of yogurt and then two berries.
7. Serve afterward.

Nutrition:

Calories 207

Fats 15.29g

Carbs 4.36g

Net Carbs 3.86g

Protein 12.91g

42. Keto Belgian Sugar Chaffles

Preparation Time: 10 minutes

Cooking Time: 24 minutes

Servings: 4

Ingredients:

- 1 egg, beaten
- 2 tbsp swerve brown sugar
- ½ tbsp butter, melted
- 1 tsp vanilla extract
- 1 cup finely grated Parmesan cheese

Directions:

1. Preheat the waffle iron.
2. Mix all the ingredients in a medium bowl.
3. Open the iron and pour in a quarter of the mixture. Close and cook until crispy, 6 minutes.
4. Remove the chaffle onto a plate and make 3 more with the remaining ingredients.
5. Cut each chaffle into wedges, plate, allow cooling and serve.

Nutrition:

Calories 136

Fats 9.45g

Carbs 3.69g

Net Carbs 3.69g

Protein 8.5g

43. Lemon and Paprika Chaffles

Preparation Time: 10 minutes

Cooking Time: 28 minutes

Servings: 4

Ingredients:

- 1 egg, beaten
- 1 oz cream cheese, softened
- 1/3 cup finely grated mozzarella cheese
- 1 tbsp almond flour
- 1 tsp butter, melted
- 1 tsp maple (sugar-free) syrup
- ½ tsp sweet paprika
- ½ tsp lemon extract

Directions:

1. Preheat the waffle iron.
2. Mix all the ingredients in a medium bowl
3. Open the iron and pour in a quarter of the mixture. Close and cook until crispy, 7 minutes.
4. Remove the chaffle onto a plate and make 3 more with the remaining mixture.
5. Cut each chaffle into wedges, plate, allow cooling and serve.

Nutrition:

Calories 48

Fats 4.22g

Carbs 0.6g

Net Carbs 0.5g

Protein 2g

44. Herby Chaffle Snacks

Preparation Time: 10 minutes

Cooking Time: 28 minutes

Servings: 4

Ingredients:

- 1 egg, beaten
- ½ cup finely grated Monterey Jack cheese
- ¼ cup finely grated Parmesan cheese
- ½ tsp dried mixed herbs

Directions:

1. Preheat the waffle iron.
2. Mix all the ingredients in a medium bowl
3. Open the iron and pour in a quarter of the mixture. Close and cook until crispy, 7 minutes.
4. Remove the chaffle onto a plate and make 3 more with the rest of the ingredients.
5. Cut each chaffle into wedges and plate.
6. Allow cooling and serve.

Nutrition:

Calories 96

Fats 6.29g

Carbs 2.19g

Net Carbs 2.19g

Protein 7.42g

45. Pumpkin Spice Chaffles

Preparation Time: 10 minutes

Cooking Time: 14 minutes

Servings: 2

Ingredients:

- 1 egg, beaten
- ½ tsp pumpkin pie spice
- ½ cup finely grated mozzarella cheese
- 1 tbsp sugar-free pumpkin puree

Directions:

1. Preheat the waffle iron.
2. In a medium bowl, mix all the ingredients.
3. Open the iron, pour in half of the batter, close, and cook until crispy, 6 to 7 minutes.
4. Remove the chaffle onto a plate and set aside.
5. Make another chaffle with the remaining batter.
6. Allow cooling and serve afterward.

Nutrition:

Calories 90

Fats 6.46g

Carbs 1.98g

Net Carbs 1.58g

Protein 5.94g

46. Breakfast Spinach Ricotta Chaffles

Preparation Time: 10 minutes

Cooking Time: 28 minutes

Servings: 4

Ingredients:

- 4 oz frozen spinach, thawed, squeezed dry
- 1 cup ricotta cheese
- 2 eggs, beaten
- ½ tsp garlic powder
- ¼ cup finely grated Pecorino Romano cheese
- ½ cup finely grated mozzarella cheese
- Salt and freshly ground black pepper to taste

Directions:

1. Preheat the waffle iron.
2. In a medium bowl, mix all the ingredients.
3. Open the iron, lightly grease with cooking spray and spoon in a quarter of the mixture.
4. Close the iron and cook until brown and crispy, 7 minutes.
5. Remove the chaffle onto a plate and set aside.
6. Make three more chaffles with the remaining mixture.
7. Allow cooling and serve afterward.

Nutrition:

Calories 188

Fats 13.15g

Carbs 5.06g

Net Carbs 4.06g

Protein 12.79g

47. Scrambled Egg Stuffed Chaffles

Preparation Time: 15 minutes

Cooking Time: 28 minutes

Servings: 4

Ingredients:

For the chaffles:

- 1 cup finely grated cheddar cheese
- 2 eggs, beaten
- For the egg stuffing:
- 1 tbsp olive oil
- 1 small red bell pepper
- 4 large eggs
- 1 small green bell pepper
- Salt and freshly ground black pepper to taste
- 2 tbsp grated Parmesan cheese

Directions:

For the chaffles:

1. Preheat the waffle iron.
2. In a medium bowl, mix the cheddar cheese and egg.
3. Open the iron, pour in a quarter of the mixture, close, and cook until crispy, 6 to 7 minutes.
4. Plate and make three more chaffles using the remaining mixture.

For the egg stuffing:

1. Meanwhile, heat the olive oil in a medium skillet over medium heat on a stovetop.
2. In a medium bowl, beat the eggs with the bell peppers, salt, black pepper, and Parmesan cheese.
3. Pour the mixture into the skillet and scramble until set to your likeness, 2 minutes.
4. Between two chaffles, spoon half of the scrambled eggs and repeat with the second set of chaffles.
5. Serve afterward.

Nutrition Facts per Serving:

Calories 387   Fats 22.52g   Carbs 18.12g

Net Carbs 17.52g   Protein 27.76g

48. Mixed Berry-Vanilla Chaffles

Preparation Time: 10 minutes

Cooking Time: 28 minutes

Servings: 4

Ingredients:

- 1 egg, beaten
- ½ cup finely grated mozzarella cheese
- 1 tbsp cream cheese, softened
- 1 tbsp sugar-free maple syrup
- 2 strawberries, sliced
- 2 raspberries, slices
- ¼ tsp blackberry extract
- ¼ tsp vanilla extract
- ½ cup plain yogurt for serving

Directions:

1. Preheat the waffle iron.
2. In a medium bowl, mix all the ingredients except the yogurt.
3. Open the iron, lightly grease with cooking spray and pour in a quarter of the mixture.
4. Close the iron and cook until golden brown and crispy, 7 minutes.
5. Remove the chaffle onto a plate and set aside.
6. Make three more chaffles with the remaining mixture.
7. To Servings: top with the yogurt and enjoy.

Nutrition Facts per Serving:

Calories 78

Fats 5.29g

Carbs 3.02g

Net Carbs 2.72g

Protein 4.32g

49. Ham and Cheddar Chaffles

Preparation Time: 15 minutes

Cooking Time: 28 minutes

Servings: 4

Ingredients:

- 1 cup finely shredded parsnips, steamed
- 8 oz ham, diced
- 2 eggs, beaten
- 1 ½ cups finely grated cheddar cheese
- ½ tsp garlic powder
- 2 tbsp chopped fresh parsley leaves
- ¼ tsp smoked paprika
- ½ tsp dried thyme
- Salt and freshly ground black pepper to taste

Directions:

1. Preheat the waffle iron.
2. In a medium bowl, mix all the ingredients.
3. Open the iron, lightly grease with cooking spray and pour in a quarter of the mixture.
4. Close the iron and cook until crispy, 7 minutes.
5. Remove the chaffle onto a plate and set aside.
6. Make three more chaffles using the remaining mixture.
7. Serve afterward.

Nutrition Facts per Serving:

Calories 506

Fats 24.05g

Carbs 30.02g

Net Carbs 28.22g

Protein 42.74g

50. Savory Gruyere and Chives Chaffles

Preparation Time: 15 minutes

Cooking Time: 14 minutes

Servings: 2

Ingredients:

- 2 eggs, beaten
- 1 cup finely grated Gruyere cheese
- 2 tbsp finely grated cheddar cheese
- 1/8 tsp freshly ground black pepper
- 3 tbsp minced fresh chives + more for garnishing
- 2 sunshine fried eggs for topping

Directions:

1. Preheat the waffle iron.
2. In a medium bowl, mix the eggs, cheeses, black pepper, and chives.
3. Open the iron and pour in half of the mixture.
4. Close the iron and cook until brown and crispy, 7 minutes.
5. Remove the chaffle onto a plate and set aside.
6. Make another chaffle using the remaining mixture.
7. Top each chaffle with one fried egg each, garnish with the chives and serve.

Nutrition Facts per Serving:

Calories 712

Fats 41.32g

Carbs 3.88g

Net Carbs 3.78g

Protein 23.75g

51. Chicken Quesadilla Chaffle

Preparation Time: 10 minutes

Cooking Time: 14 minutes

Servings: 2

Ingredients:

- 1 egg, beaten
- ¼ tsp taco seasoning
- 1/3 cup finely grated cheddar cheese
- 1/3 cup cooked chopped chicken

Directions:

1. Preheat the waffle iron.
2. In a medium bowl, mix the eggs, taco seasoning, and cheddar cheese. Add the chicken and combine well.
3. Open the iron, lightly grease with cooking spray and pour in half of the mixture.
4. Close the iron and cook until brown and crispy, 7 minutes.
5. Remove the chaffle onto a plate and set aside.
6. Make another chaffle using the remaining mixture.
7. Serve afterward.

Nutrition Facts per Serving:

Calories 314

Fats 20.64g

Carbs 5.71g

Net Carbs 5.71g

Protein 16.74g

52. Hot Chocolate Breakfast Chaffle

Preparation Time: 10 minutes

Cooking Time: 14 minutes

Servings: 2

Ingredients:

- 1 egg, beaten
- 2 tbsp almond flour
- 1 tbsp unsweetened cocoa powder
- 2 tbsp cream cheese, softened
- ¼ cup finely grated Monterey Jack cheese
- 2 tbsp sugar-free maple syrup
- 1 tsp vanilla extract

Directions:

1. Preheat the waffle iron.
2. In a medium bowl, mix all the ingredients.
3. Open the iron, lightly grease with cooking spray and pour in half of the mixture.
4. Close the iron and cook until crispy, 7 minutes.
5. Remove the chaffle onto a plate and set aside.
6. Pour the remaining batter in the iron and make the second chaffle.
7. Allow cooling and serve afterward.

Nutrition Facts per Serving:

Calories 47

Fats 3.67g

Carbs 1.39g

Net Carbs 0.89g

Protein 2.29g

53. Blueberry Chaffles

Preparation Time: 15 minutes

Servings: 4

Ingredients:

- 2 eggs
- 1/2 cup blueberries
- 1/2 tsp baking powder
- 1/2 tsp vanilla
- 2 tsp Swerve
- 3 tbsp almond flour
- 1 cup mozzarella cheese, shredded

Directions:

1. Preheat your waffle maker.
2. In a medium bowl, mix eggs, vanilla, Swerve, almond flour, and cheese.
3. Add blueberries and stir well.
4. Spray waffle maker with cooking spray.
5. Pour 1/4 batter in the hot waffle maker and cook for 5-8 minutes or until golden brown. Repeat with the remaining batter.
6. Serve and enjoy.

Nutrition:

Calories 96

Fat 6.1 g

Carbohydrates 5.7 g

Sugar 2.2 g

Protein 6.1 g

Cholesterol 86 mg

54. Pecan Pumpkin Chaffle

Preparation Time: 15 minutes

Servings: 2

Ingredients:

- 1 egg
- 2 tbsp pecans, toasted and chopped
- 2 tbsp almond flour
- 1 tsp erythritol
- 1/4 tsp pumpkin pie spice
- 1 tbsp pumpkin puree
- 1/2 cup mozzarella cheese, grated

Directions:

1. Preheat your waffle maker.
2. Beat egg in a small bowl.
3. Add remaining ingredients and mix well.
4. Spray waffle maker with cooking spray.
5. Pour half batter in the hot waffle maker and cook for 5 minutes or until golden brown. Repeat with the remaining batter.
6. Serve and enjoy.

Nutrition:

Calories 121

Fat 9.7 g

Carbohydrates 5.7 g

Sugar 3.3 g

Protein 6.7 g

Cholesterol 86 mg

55. Pumpkin Cheesecake Chaffle

Preparation Time: 15 minutes

Servings: 2

Ingredients:

For chaffle:

- 1 egg
- 1/2 tsp vanilla
- 1/2 tsp baking powder, gluten-free
- 1/4 tsp pumpkin spice
- 1 tsp cream cheese, softened
- 2 tsp heavy cream
- 1 tbsp Swerve

- 1 tbsp almond flour
- 2 tsp pumpkin puree
- 1/2 cup mozzarella cheese, shredded

For filling:

- 1/4 tsp vanilla
- 1 tbsp Swerve
- 2 tbsp cream cheese

Directions:

1. Preheat your mini waffle maker.
2. In a small bowl, mix all chaffle ingredients.
3. Spray waffle maker with cooking spray.
4. Pour half batter in the hot waffle maker and cook for 3-5 minutes. Repeat with the remaining batter.
5. In a small bowl, combine all filling ingredients.
6. Spread filling mixture between two chaffles and place in the fridge for 10 minutes.
7. Serve and enjoy.

Nutrition:

Calories 107

Fat 7.2 g

Carbohydrates 5 g

Sugar 0.7 g

Protein 6.7 g

Cholesterol 93 mg

56. Quick & Easy Blueberry Chaffle

Preparation Time: 15 minutes

Servings: 2

Ingredients:

- 1 egg, lightly beaten
- 1/4 cup blueberries
- 1/2 tsp vanilla
- 1 oz cream cheese
- 1/4 tsp baking powder, gluten-free
- 4 tsp Swerve
- 1 tbsp coconut flour

Directions:

1. Preheat your waffle maker.
2. In a small bowl, mix coconut flour, baking powder, and Swerve until well combined.
3. Add vanilla, cream cheese, egg, and vanilla and whisk until combined.
4. Spray waffle maker with cooking spray.
5. Pour half batter in the hot waffle maker and top with 4-5 blueberries and cook for 4-5 minutes until golden brown. Repeat with the remaining batter.
6. Serve and enjoy.

Nutrition:

Calories 135

Fat 8.2 g

Carbohydrates 11 g

Sugar 2.6 g

Protein 5 g

Cholesterol 97 mg

57. Apple Cinnamon Chaffles

Preparation Time: 20 minutes

Servings: 3

Ingredients:

- 3 eggs, lightly beaten
- 1 cup mozzarella cheese, shredded
- ¼ cup apple, chopped
- ½ tsp monk fruit sweetener
- 1 ½ tsp cinnamon
- ¼ tsp baking powder, gluten-free
- 2 tbsp coconut flour

Directions:

1. Preheat your waffle maker.
2. Add remaining ingredients and stir until well combined.
3. Spray waffle maker with cooking spray.
4. Pour 1/3 of batter in the hot waffle maker and cook for 4 minutes or until golden brown. Repeat with the remaining batter.
5. Serve and enjoy.

Nutrition:

Calories 142

Fat 7.4 g

Carbohydrates 9.7 g

Sugar 3 g

Protein 9.6 g

Cholesterol 169 mg

58. Cinnamon Cream Cheese Chaffle

Preparation Time: 15 minutes

Servings: 2

Ingredients:

- 2 eggs, lightly beaten
- 1 tsp collagen
- ¼ tsp baking powder, gluten-free
- 1 tsp monk fruit sweetener
- ½ tsp cinnamon
- ¼ cup cream cheese, softened
- Pinch of salt

Directions:

1. Preheat your waffle maker.
2. Add all ingredients into the bowl and beat using hand mixer until well combined.
3. Spray waffle maker with cooking spray.
4. Pour 1/2 batter in the hot waffle maker and cook for 3-4 minutes or until golden brown. Repeat with the remaining batter.
5. Serve and enjoy.

Nutrition:

Calories 179

Fat 14.5 g

Carbohydrates 1.9 g

Sugar 0.4 g

Protein 10.8 g

Cholesterol 196 mg

59. Mozzarella Peanut Butter Chaffle

Preparation Time: 15 minutes

Servings: 2

Ingredients:

- 1 egg, lightly beaten
- 2 tbsp peanut butter
- 2 tbsp Swerve
- 1/2 cup mozzarella cheese, shredded

Directions:

1. Preheat your waffle maker.
2. In a bowl, mix egg, cheese, Swerve, and peanut butter until well combined.
3. Spray waffle maker with cooking spray.
4. Pour half batter in the hot waffle maker and cook for 4 minutes or until golden brown. Repeat with the remaining batter.
5. Serve and enjoy.

Nutrition:

Calories 150

Fat 11.5 g

Carbohydrates 5.6 g

Sugar 1.7 g

Protein 8.8 g

Cholesterol 86 mg

60. Choco Chip Pumpkin Chaffle

Preparation Time: 15 minutes

Servings: 2

Ingredients:

- 1 egg, lightly beaten
- 1 tbsp almond flour
- 1 tbsp unsweetened chocolate chips
- 1/4 tsp pumpkin pie spice
- 2 tbsp Swerve
- 1 tbsp pumpkin puree
- 1/2 cup mozzarella cheese, shredded

Directions:

1. Preheat your waffle maker.
2. In a small bowl, mix egg and pumpkin puree.
3. Add pumpkin pie spice, Swerve, almond flour, and cheese and mix well.
4. Stir in chocolate chips.
5. Spray waffle maker with cooking spray.
6. Pour half batter in the hot waffle maker and cook for 4 minutes. Repeat with the remaining batter.
7. Serve and enjoy.

Nutrition:

Calories 130

Fat 9.2 g

Carbohydrates 5.9 g

Sugar 0.6 g

Protein 6.6 g

Cholesterol 86 mg

61. Maple Chaffle

Preparation Time: 15 minutes

Servings: 2

Ingredients:

- 1 egg, lightly beaten
- 2 egg whites
- 1/2 tsp maple extract
- 2 tsp Swerve
- 1/2 tsp baking powder, gluten-free
- 2 tbsp almond milk
- 2 tbsp coconut flour

Directions:

1. Preheat your waffle maker.
2. In a bowl, whip egg whites until stiff peaks form.
3. Stir in maple extract, Swerve, baking powder, almond milk, coconut flour, and egg.
4. Spray waffle maker with cooking spray.
5. Pour half batter in the hot waffle maker and cook for 3-5 minutes or until golden brown. Repeat with the remaining batter.
6. Serve and enjoy.

Nutrition:

Calories 122

Fat 6.6 g

Carbohydrates 9 g

Sugar 1 g

Protein 7.7 g

Cholesterol 82 mg

62. Sweet Vanilla Chocolate Chaffle

Preparation Time: 10 minutes

Servings: 1

Ingredients:

- 1 egg, lightly beaten
- 1/4 tsp cinnamon
- 1/2 tsp vanilla
- 1 tbsp Swerve
- 2 tsp unsweetened cocoa powder
- 1 tbsp coconut flour
- 2 oz cream cheese, softened

Directions:

1. Add all ingredients into the small bowl and mix until well combined.
2. Spray waffle maker with cooking spray.
3. Pour batter in the hot waffle maker and cook until golden brown.
4. Serve and enjoy.

Nutrition:

Calories 312

Fat 25.4 g

Carbohydrates 11.5 g

Sugar 0.8 g

Protein 11.6 g

Cholesterol 226 mg

63. Choco Chip Lemon Chaffle

Preparation Time: 15 minutes

Servings: 2

Ingredients:

- 2 eggs, lightly beaten
- 1 tbsp unsweetened chocolate chips
- 2 tsp Swerve
- 1/2 tsp vanilla
- 1/2 tsp lemon extract
- 1/2 cup mozzarella cheese, shredded
- 2 tsp almond flour

Directions:

1. Preheat your waffle maker.
2. In a bowl, whisk eggs, Swerve, vanilla, lemon extract, cheese, and almond flour.
3. Add chocolate chips and stir well.
4. Spray waffle maker with cooking spray.
5. Pour 1/2 of the batter in the hot waffle maker and cook for 4-5 minutes or until golden brown. Repeat with the remaining batter.
6. Serve and enjoy.

Nutrition:

Calories 157

Fat 10.8 g

Carbohydrates 5.4 g

Sugar 0.7 g

Protein 9 g

Cholesterol 167 mg

64. Peanut Butter Sandwich Chaffle

Preparation Time: 15 minutes

Servings: 1

Ingredients:

For chaffle:

- 1 egg, lightly beaten
- 1/2 cup mozzarella cheese, shredded
- 1/4 tsp espresso powder
- 1 tbsp unsweetened chocolate chips
- 1 tbsp Swerve
- 2 tbsp unsweetened cocoa powder

For filling:

- 1 tbsp butter, softened
- 2 tbsp Swerve
- 3 tbsp creamy peanut butter

Directions:

1. Preheat your waffle maker.
2. In a bowl, whisk together egg, espresso powder, chocolate chips, Swerve, and cocoa powder.
3. Add mozzarella cheese and stir well.
4. Spray waffle maker with cooking spray.
5. Pour 1/2 of the batter in the hot waffle maker and cook for 3-4 minutes or until golden brown. Repeat with the remaining batter.
6. For filling: In a small bowl, stir together butter, Swerve, and peanut butter until smooth.
7. Once chaffles is cool, then spread filling mixture between two chaffle and place in the fridge for 10 minutes.
8. Cut chaffle sandwich in half and serve.

Nutrition:

Calories 190

Fat 16.1 g

Carbohydrates 9.6 g

Sugar 1.1 g

Protein 8.2 g

Cholesterol 101 mg

65. Cherry Chocolate Chaffle

Preparation Time: 10 minutes

Servings: 1

Ingredients:

- 1 egg, lightly beaten
- 1 tbsp unsweetened chocolate chips
- 2 tbsp sugar-free cherry pie filling
- 2 tbsp heavy whipping cream
- 1/2 cup mozzarella cheese, shredded
- 1/2 tsp baking powder, gluten-free
- 1 tbsp Swerve
- 1 tbsp unsweetened cocoa powder
- 1 tbsp almond flour

Directions:

1. Preheat the waffle maker.
2. In a bowl, whisk together egg, cheese, baking powder, Swerve, cocoa powder, and almond flour.
3. Spray waffle maker with cooking spray.
4. Pour batter in the hot waffle maker and cook until golden brown.
5. Top with cherry pie filling, heavy whipping cream, and chocolate chips and serve.

Nutrition:

Calories 264

Fat 22 g

Carbohydrates 8.5 g

Sugar 0.5 g

Protein 12.7 g

Cholesterol 212 mg

66. Pumpkin Chaffle with Frosting

Preparation Time: 15 minutes

Servings: 2

Ingredients:

- 1 egg, lightly beaten
- 1 tbsp sugar-free pumpkin puree
- 1/4 tsp pumpkin pie spice
- 1/2 cup mozzarella cheese, shredded

For frosting:

- 1/2 tsp vanilla
- 2 tbsp Swerve
- 2 tbsp cream cheese, softened

Directions:

1. Preheat your waffle maker.
2. Add egg in a bowl and whisk well.
3. Add pumpkin puree, pumpkin pie spice, and cheese and stir well.
4. Spray waffle maker with cooking spray.
5. Pour 1/2 of the batter in the hot waffle maker and cook for 3-4 minutes or until golden brown. Repeat with the remaining batter.
6. In a small bowl, mix all frosting ingredients until smooth.
7. Add frosting on top of hot chaffles and serve.

Nutrition:

Calories 98

Fat 7 g

Carbohydrates 3.6 g

Sugar 0.6 g

Protein 5.6 g

Cholesterol 97 mg

67. Breakfast Peanut Butter Chaffle

Preparation Time: 15 minutes

Servings: 2

Ingredients:

- 1 egg, lightly beaten
- ½ tsp vanilla
- 1 tbsp Swerve
- 2 tbsp powdered peanut butter
- ½ cup mozzarella cheese, shredded

Directions:

1. Preheat your waffle maker.
2. Add all ingredients into the bowl and mix until well combined.
3. Spray waffle maker with cooking spray.
4. Pour half batter in the hot waffle maker and cook for 5-7 minutes or until golden brown. Repeat with the remaining batter.
5. Serve and enjoy.

Nutrition:

Calories 80

Fat 4.1 g

Carbohydrates 2.9 g

Sugar 0.6 g

Protein 7.4 g

Cholesterol 86 mg

68. Chaffles with Caramelized Apples and Yogurt

Serving: 2

Preparation Time: 5 minutes

Cooking Time: 10 minutes

Ingredients

- 1 tablespoon unsalted butter
- 1 tablespoon golden brown sugar
- 1 Granny Smith apple, cored and thinly sliced
- 1 pinch salt
- 2 whole-grain frozen waffles, toasted
- 1/2 cup mozzarella cheese, shredded
- 1/4 cup Yoplait® Original French Vanilla yogurt

Direction

1. Melt the butter in a large skillet over medium-high heat until starting to brown. Add mozzarella cheese and stir well.
2. Add the sugar, apple slices and salt and cook, stirring frequently, until apples are softened and tender, about 6 to 9 minutes.
3. Put one warm waffle each on a plate, top each with yogurt and apples. Serve warm.

Nutrition:

Calories: 240 calories

Total Fat: 10.4 g

Cholesterol: 54 mg

Sodium: 226 mg

Total Carbohydrate: 33.8 g

Protein: 4.7 g

69. Chaffle Ice Cream Bowl

Preparation Time: 5 minutes

Cooking Time: 0 minutes

Servings: 2

Ingredients:

- 4 basic chaffles
- 2 scoops keto ice cream
- 2 teaspoons sugar-free chocolate syrup

Method:

1. Arrange 2 basic chaffles in a bowl, following the contoured design of the bowl.
2. Top with the ice cream.
3. Drizzle with the syrup on top.
4. Serve.

Nutritional Value:

- Calories 181
- Total Fat 17.2g
- Saturated Fat 4.2g
- Cholesterol 26mg
- Sodium 38mg
- Total Carbohydrate 7g
- Dietary Fiber 1g
- Total Sugars 4.1g
- Protein 0.4g
- Potassium 0mg

70. Zucchini Chaffle

Preparation Time: 10 minutes

Cooking Time: 8 minutes

Servings: 2

Ingredients:

- 1 cup zucchini, grated
- ¼ cup mozzarella cheese, shredded
- 1 egg, beaten
- ½ cup Parmesan cheese, shredded
- 1 teaspoon dried basil
- Salt and pepper to taste

Method:

1. Preheat your waffle maker.
2. Sprinkle pinch of salt over the zucchini and mix.
3. Let sit for 2 minutes.
4. Wrap zucchini with paper towel and squeeze to get rid of water.
5. Transfer to a bowl and stir in the rest of the ingredients.
6. Pour half of the mixture into the waffle maker.
7. Close the device.
8. Cook for 4 minutes.
9. Make the second chaffle following the same steps.

Nutritional Value:

- Calories 194
- Total Fat 13 g
- Saturated Fat 7 g
- Cholesterol 115 mg
- Sodium 789 mg
- Potassium 223 mg
- Total Carbohydrate 4 g
- Dietary Fiber 1 g
- Protein 16 g
- Total Sugars 2 g

71. Chaffle Cream Cake

Preparation Time: 20 minutes

Cooking Time: 30 minutes

Servings: 8

Ingredients:

Chaffle

- 4 oz. cream cheese
- 4 eggs
- 1 tablespoon butter, melted
- 1 teaspoon vanilla extract
- ½ teaspoon cinnamon
- 1 tablespoon sweetener
- 4 tablespoons coconut flour
- 1 tablespoon almond flour
- 1 ½ teaspoons baking powder
- 1 tablespoon coconut flakes (sugar-free)
- 1 tablespoon walnuts, chopped

Frosting

- 2 oz. cream cheese
- 2 tablespoons butter
- 2 tablespoons sweetener
- ½ teaspoon vanilla

Method:

1. Combine all the chaffle ingredients except coconut flakes and walnuts in a blender.
2. Blend until smooth.
3. Plug in your waffle maker.
4. Add some of the mixture to the waffle maker.
5. Cook for 3 minutes.
6. Repeat steps until the remaining batter is used.
7. While letting the chaffles cool, make the frosting by combining all the ingredients.
8. Use a mixer to combine and turn frosting into fluffy consistency.
9. Spread the frosting on top of the chaffles.

Nutritional Value:

- Calories127
- Total Fat 13.7g
- Saturated Fat 9 g
- Cholesterol 102.9mg
- Sodium 107.3mg
- Potassium 457 mg
- Total Carbohydrate 5.5g
- Dietary Fiber 1.3g
- Protein 5.3g
- Total Sugars 1.5g

72. Taco Chaffle

Preparation Time: 15 minutes

Cooking Time: 20 minutes

Servings: 4

Ingredients:

- 1 tablespoon olive oil
- 1 lb. ground beef
- 1 teaspoon ground cumin
- 1 teaspoon chili powder
- ¼ teaspoon onion powder
- ½ teaspoon garlic powder
- Salt to taste
- 4 basic chaffles
- 1 cup cabbage, chopped
- 4 tablespoons salsa (sugar-free)

Method:

1. Pour the olive oil into a pan over medium heat.
2. Add the ground beef.
3. Season with the salt and spices.
4. Cook until brown and crumbly.
5. Fold the chaffle to create a "taco shell".
6. Stuff each chaffle taco with cabbage.
7. Top with the ground beef and salsa.

Nutritional Value:

- Calories 255
- Total Fat 10.9g
- Saturated Fat 3.2g
- Cholesterol 101mg
- Sodium 220mg
- Potassium 561mg
- Total Carbohydrate 3g
- Dietary Fiber 1g
- Protein 35.1g
- Total Sugars 1.3g

73. Chicken Parmesan Chaffle

Preparation Time: 15 minutes

Cooking Time: 8 minutes

Servings: 2

Ingredients:

Chaffle

- 1 egg, beaten
- ¼ cup cheddar cheese, shredded
- 1/8 cup Parmesan cheese, grated
- 1 teaspoon cream cheese
- ½ cup chicken breast meat, shredded
- 1/8 teaspoon garlic powder
- 1 teaspoon Italian seasoning

Toppings

- 1 tablespoon pizza sauce (sugar-free)
- 2 provolone cheese slices

Method:

1. Plug in your waffle maker.
2. Combine all the chaffle ingredients in a bowl.
3. Mix well.
4. Add half of the mixture to the waffle maker.
5. Cook for 4 minutes.
6. Repeat with the next chaffle.
7. Spread the pizza sauce on top of each chaffle and put Provolone on top.

Nutritional Value:

- Calories 125
- Total Fat 8.3g
- Saturated Fat 4 g
- Cholesterol 115.3mg
- Sodium 285.7mg
- Potassium 760 mg
- Total Carbohydrate 2.6g
- Dietary Fiber 0.3g
- Protein 9.4g

74. Cheese Garlic Chaffle

Preparation Time: 10 minutes

Cooking Time: 8 minutes

Servings: 2

Ingredients:

Chaffle

- 1 egg
- 1 teaspoon cream cheese
- ½ cup mozzarella cheese, shredded
- ½ teaspoon garlic powder
- 1 teaspoon Italian seasoning

Topping

- 1 tablespoon butter
- ½ teaspoon garlic powder
- ½ teaspoon Italian seasoning
- 2 tablespoon mozzarella cheese, shredded

Method:

1. Plug in your waffle maker to preheat.
2. Preheat your oven to 350 degrees F.
3. In a bowl, combine all the chaffle ingredients.
4. Cook in the waffle maker for 4 minutes per chaffle.
5. Transfer to a baking pan.
6. Spread butter on top of each chaffle.
7. Sprinkle garlic powder and Italian seasoning on top.
8. Top with mozzarella cheese.
9. Bake until the cheese has melted.

Nutritional Value:

- Calories141
- Total Fat 13 g
- Saturated Fat 8 g
- Cholesterol 115.8 mg
- Sodium 255.8 mg
- Potassium 350 mg
- Total Carbohydrate 2.6g
- Dietary Fiber 0.7g

75. Chicken Chaffle Sandwich

Preparation Time: 5 minutes

Cooking Time: 15 minutes

Servings: 2

Ingredients:

- 1 chicken breast fillet, sliced into strips
- Salt and pepper to taste
- 1 teaspoon dried rosemary
- 1 tablespoon olive oil
- 4 basic chaffles
- 2 tablespoons butter, melted
- 2 tablespoons Parmesan cheese, grated

Method:

1. Season the chicken strips with salt, pepper and rosemary.
2. Add olive oil to a pan over medium low heat.
3. Cook the chicken until brown on both sides.
4. Spread butter on top of each chaffle.
5. Sprinkle cheese on top.
6. Place the chicken on top and top with another chaffle.

Nutritional Value:

- Calories 262
- Total Fat 20g
- Saturated Fat 9.2g
- Cholesterol 77mg
- Sodium 270mg
- Potassium 125mg
- Total Carbohydrate 1g
- Dietary Fiber 0.2g
- Protein 20.2g
- Total Sugars 0g

76. Cornbread Chaffle

Preparation Time: 5 minutes

Cooking Time: 8 minutes

Servings: 2

Ingredients:

- 1 egg, beaten
- ½ cup cheddar cheese, shredded
- 5 slices pickled jalapeno, chopped and drained
- 1 teaspoon hot sauce
- ¼ teaspoon corn extract
- Salt to taste

Method:

1. Combine all the ingredients in a bowl while preheating your waffle maker.
2. Add half of the mixture to the device.
3. Seal and cook for 4 minutes.
4. Let cool on a plate for 2 minutes.
5. Repeat steps for the second chaffle.

Nutritional Value:

- Calories150
- Total Fat 11.8g
- Saturated Fat 7 g
- Cholesterol 121mg
- Sodium 1399.4mg
- Potassium 350 mg
- Total Carbohydrate 1.1g
- Dietary Fiber 0g
- Protein 9.6g
- Total Sugars 0.2g

77. Italian Sausage Chaffles

Preparation Time: 5 minutes

Cooking Time: 8 minutes

Servings: 2

Ingredients:

- 1 egg, beaten
- 1 cup cheddar cheese, shredded
- ¼ cup Parmesan cheese, grated
- 1 lb. Italian sausage, crumbled
- 2 teaspoons baking powder
- 1 cup almond flour

Method:

1. Preheat your waffle maker.
2. Mix all the ingredients in a bowl.
3. Pour half of the mixture into the waffle maker.
4. Cover and cook for 4 minutes.
5. Transfer to a plate.
6. Let cool to make it crispy.
7. Do the same steps to make the next chaffle.

Nutritional Value:

- Calories 332
- Total Fat 27.1g
- Saturated Fat 10.2g
- Cholesterol 98mg
- Sodium 634mg
- Total Carbohydrate 1.9g
- Dietary Fiber 0.5g
- Total Sugars 0.1g
- Protein 19.6g
- Potassium 359mg

78. LT Chaffle Sandwich

Preparation Time: 10 minutes

Cooking Time: 15 minutes

Servings: 2

Ingredients:

- Cooking spray
- 4 slices bacon
- 1 tablespoon mayonnaise
- 4 basic chaffles
- 2 lettuce leaves
- 2 tomato slices

Method:

1. Coat your pan with foil and place it over medium heat.
2. Cook the bacon until golden and crispy.
3. Spread mayo on top of the chaffle.
4. Top with the lettuce, bacon and tomato.
5. Top with another chaffle.

Nutritional Value:

- Calories 238
- Total Fat 18.4g
- Saturated Fat 5.6g
- Cholesterol 44mg
- Sodium 931mg
- Potassium 258mg
- Total Carbohydrate 3g
- Dietary Fiber 0.2g
- Protein 14.3g
- Total Sugars 0.9g

79. Sloppy Joe Chaffle

Preparation Time: 15 minutes

Cooking Time: 15 minutes

Servings: 2

Ingredients:

- 1 teaspoon olive oil
- 1 lb. ground beef
- Salt and pepper to taste
- 1 teaspoon onion powder
- 1 teaspoon garlic powder
- 3 tablespoons tomato paste
- 1 tablespoon chili powder
- 1 teaspoon mustard powder
- ½ teaspoon paprika
- ½ cup beef broth
- 1 teaspoon coconut aminos
- 1 teaspoon sweetener
- 4 cornbread chaffles

Method:

1. Pour the olive oil into a pan over medium high heat.
2. Add the ground beef.
3. Season with salt, pepper and spices.
4. Cook for 5 minutes, stirring occasionally.
5. Stir in the beef broth, coconut aminos and sweetener.
6. Reduce heat and simmer for 10 minutes.
7. Top the cornbread chaffle with the ground beef mixture.
8. Top with another chaffle.

Nutritional Value:

- Calories 334
- Total Fat 12.1g
- Saturated Fat 4g
- Cholesterol 135mg
- Sodium 269mg
- Potassium 887mg
- Total Carbohydrate 6.5g
- Dietary Fiber 2g
- Protein 48.2g
- Total Sugars 2.9g

80. Peanut Butter Chaffle Cake

Preparation Time: 10 minutes

Cooking Time: 10 minutes

Servings: 2

Ingredients:

Chaffle

- 1 egg, beaten
- ¼ teaspoon baking powder
- 2 tablespoons peanut butter powder (sugar-free)
- ¼ teaspoon peanut butter extract
- 1 tablespoon heavy whipping cream
- 2 tablespoons sweetener

Frosting

- 2 tablespoons sweetener
- 1 tablespoon butter
- 1 tablespoon peanut butter (sugar-free)
- 2 tablespoons cream cheese
- ¼ teaspoon vanilla

Method:

1. Preheat your waffle maker.
2. In a large bowl, combine all the ingredients for the chaffle.
3. Pour half of the mixture into the waffle maker.
4. Seal and cook for 4 minutes.
5. Repeat steps to make the second chaffle.
6. While letting the chaffles cool, add the frosting ingredients in a bowl.
7. Use a mixer to turn mixture into fluffy frosting.
8. Spread the frosting on top of the chaffles and serve.

Nutritional Value:

- Calories192
- Total Fat 17 g
- Saturated Fat 8 g
- Cholesterol 97.1 mg
- Sodium 64.3 mg
- Potassium 342 mg
- Total Carbohydrate 3.6 g
- Dietary Fiber 0.6 g
- Protein 5.5 g
- Total Sugars 1.8 g

81. Garlic Cauliflower Chaffle

Preparation Time: 5 minutes

Cooking Time: 8 minutes

Servings: 2

Ingredients:

- 1 egg, beaten
- 1 cup cauliflower rice
- ½ cup cheddar cheese, shredded
- 1 teaspoon garlic powder

Method:

1. Plug in your waffle maker.
2. Mix all the ingredients in a bowl.
3. Transfer half of the mixture to the waffle maker.
4. Close the device and cook for 4 minutes.
5. Put the chaffle on a plate to cool for 2 minutes.
6. Repeat procedure to make the next chaffle.

Nutritional Value:

- Calories 178
- Total Fat 12.5g
- Saturated Fat 7g
- Cholesterol 112mg
- Sodium 267mg
- Total Carbohydrate 4.9g
- Dietary Fiber 0.1g
- Total Sugars 2.7g
- Protein 12g
- Potassium 73mg

82. Apple Pie Chaffle

Preparation Time: 5 minutes

Cooking Time: 8 minutes

Servings: 2

Ingredients:

- 1 egg
- ½ cup mozzarella cheese
- 1 teaspoon apple pie spice
- 1 tablespoon chocolate chips (sugar-free)

Method:

1. Mix all the ingredients in a bowl while the waffle maker is preheating.
2. Add half of the mixture into the waffle maker.
3. Seal. Cook for 4 minutes.
4. Put the chaffle on a plate to cool for 2 minutes.
5. Repeat the steps to cook the second chaffle.

Nutritional Value:

- Calories 165
- Total Fat 10.2g
- Saturated Fat 5.2g
- Cholesterol 174mg
- Sodium 156mg
- Total Carbohydrate 8.3g
- Dietary Fiber 0.6g
- Total Sugars 5.9g
- Protein 10.4g
- Potassium 109mg

83. Basic Chaffle

Preparation Time: 5 minutes

Cooking Time: 8 minutes

Serving: 2

Ingredients:

- Cooking spray
- 1 egg
- ½ cup cheddar cheese, shredded

Method:

1. Turn your waffle maker on.
2. Grease both sides with cooking spray.
3. Beat the egg in a bowl.
4. Stir in the cheddar cheese.
5. Pour half of the batter into the waffle maker.
6. Seal and cook for 4 minutes.
7. Remove the chaffle slowly from the waffle maker.
8. Let sit for 3 minutes.
9. Pour the remaining batter into the waffle maker and repeat the steps.

Nutritional Value:

- Calories 191
- Total Fat 23 g
- Saturated Fat 14 g
- Cholesterol 223 mg
- Sodium 413 mg
- Potassium 116 mg
- Total Carbohydrate 1 g
- Dietary Fiber 1 g
- Protein 20 g
- Total Sugars 1 g

84. Keto Chaffle with Almond Flour

Preparation Time: 5 minutes

Cooking Time: 8 minutes

Servings: 2

Ingredients:

- 1 egg, beaten
- ½ cup cheddar cheese, shredded
- 1 tablespoon almond flour

Method:

1. Turn on your waffle maker.
2. Mix all the ingredients in a bowl.
3. Pour half of the batter into the waffle maker.
4. Close the device and cook for 4 minutes.
5. Remove from the waffle maker.
6. Let sit for 2 to 3 minutes.
7. Repeat the steps with the remaining batter.

Nutritional Value:

- Calories 145
- Total Fat 11 g
- Saturated Fat 7 g
- Cholesterol 112 mg
- Sodium 207 mg
- Potassium 158 mg
- Total Carbohydrate 1 g
- Dietary Fiber 1 g
- Protein 10 g
- Total Sugars 1 g

85. Garlic Chaffle

Preparation Time: 5 minutes

Cooking Time: 8 minutes

Serving: 2

Ingredients:

- 1 egg
- ½ cup cheddar cheese, beaten
- 1 teaspoon coconut flour
- Pinch garlic powder

Method:

1. Plug in your waffle maker.
2. Beat the egg in a bowl.
3. Stir in the rest of the ingredients.
4. Pour half of the batter into your waffle maker.
5. Cook for 4 minutes.
6. Remove the waffle and let sit for 2 minutes.
7. Do the same steps with the remaining batter.

Nutritional Value:

- Calories 170
- Total Fat 14 g
- Saturated Fat 6 g
- Cholesterol 121 mg
- Sodium 220 mg
- Potassium 165 mg
- Total Carbohydrate 2 g
- Dietary Fiber 1 g
- Protein 10 g
- Total Sugars 1 g

86. Bacon Chaffle

Preparation Time: 5 minutes

Cooking Time: 8 minutes

Servings: 2

Ingredients:

- 1 egg
- ½ cup cheddar cheese, shredded
- 1 teaspoon baking powder
- 2 tablespoons almond flour
- 3 tablespoons bacon bits, cooked

Method:

1. Turn your waffle maker on.
2. Beat the egg in a bowl.
3. Stir in the cheese, baking powder, almond flour and bacon bits.
4. Pour half of the batter into the waffle maker.
5. Close the device.
6. Cook for 4 minutes.
7. Open and transfer waffle on a plate. Let cool for 2 minutes.
8. Repeat the same procedure with the remaining batter.

Nutritional Value:

- Calories 147
- Total Fat 11.5 g
- Saturated Fat 5.4 g
- Cholesterol 88 mg
- Sodium 286 mg
- Potassium 243 mg
- Total Carbohydrate 1.7 g
- Dietary Fiber 1 g
- Protein 9.8 g
- Total Sugars 1 g

87. Blueberry Chaffle

Preparation Time: 10 minutes

Cooking Time: 8 minutes

Servings: 2

Ingredients:

- 1 egg, beaten
- ½ cup mozzarella cheese, shredded
- 1 teaspoon baking powder
- 2 tablespoons almond flour
- 2 teaspoons sweetener
- ¼ cup blueberries, chopped

Method:

1. Combine all the ingredients in a bowl. Mix well.
2. Turn on the waffle maker.
3. Pour half of the mixture into the cooking device.
4. Close it and cook for 4 minutes.
5. Open the waffle maker and transfer to a plate.
6. Let cool for 2 minutes.
7. Add the remaining mixture to the waffle maker and repeat the steps.

Nutritional Value:

- Calories 175
- Total Fat 4.3g
- Saturated Fat 1.5g
- Cholesterol 86mg
- Sodium 76mg
- Potassium 296mg
- Total Carbohydrate 6.6g
- Dietary Fiber 1.7g
- Protein 5.3g
- Total Sugars 2g

88. Cinnamon Chaffle

Preparation Time: 5 minutes

Cooking Time: 8 minutes

Servings: 2

Ingredients:

- 1 egg
- ½ cup of mozzarella cheese, shredded
- 2 tablespoons almond flour
- 1 teaspoon baking powder
- 1 teaspoon vanilla
- 2 teaspoons cinnamon
- 1 teaspoon sweetener

Method:

1. Preheat your waffle maker.
2. Beat the egg in a bowl.
3. Stir in the rest of the ingredients.
4. Transfer half of the batter into the waffle maker.
5. Close and cook for 4 minutes.
6. Open and put the waffle on a plate. Let cool for 2 minutes.
7. Do the same steps for the remaining batter.

Nutritional Value:

- Calories 136
- Total Fat 7.4g
- Saturated Fat 2.9g
- Cholesterol 171mg
- Sodium 152mg
- Potassium 590mg
- Total Carbohydrate 9.6g
- Dietary Fiber 3.6g
- Protein 9.9g
- Total Sugars 1g

89. Nut Butter Chaffle

Preparation Time: 10 minutes

Cooking Time: 8 minutes

Servings: 2

Ingredients:

- 1 egg
- ½ cup mozzarella cheese, shredded
- 2 tablespoons almond flour
- ½ teaspoon baking powder
- 1 tablespoon sweetener
- 1 teaspoon vanilla
- 2 tablespoons nut butter

Method:

1. Turn on the waffle maker.
2. Beat the egg in a bowl and combine with the cheese.
3. In another bowl, mix the almond flour, baking powder and sweetener.
4. In the third bowl, blend the vanilla extract and nut butter.
5. Gradually add the almond flour mixture into the egg mixture.
6. Then, stir in the vanilla extract.
7. Pour the batter into the waffle maker.
8. Cook for 4 minutes.
9. Transfer to a plate and let cool for 2 minutes.
10. Repeat the steps with the remaining batter.

Nutritional Value:

- Calories 168
- Total Fat 15.5g
- Saturated Fat 3.9g
- Cholesterol 34mg
- Sodium 31mg
- Potassium 64mg
- Total Carbohydrate 1.6g
- Dietary Fiber 1.4g
- Protein 5.4g
- Total Sugars 0.6g

Expert

90. Lemon Chaffle

Preparation Time: 10 minutes

Cooking Time: 12 minutes

Servings: 3-4

Ingredients:

- 1 egg
- ¼ cup mozzarella cheese, shredded
- 1 oz. cream cheese
- 2 teaspoons lemon juice
- 2 tablespoons sweetener
- 1 teaspoon baking powder
- 4 tablespoons almond flour

Method:

1. Preheat your waffle maker.
2. Beat the egg in a bowl.
3. Stir in the two cheeses.
4. Add the remaining ingredients.
5. Mix well.
6. Pour batter into the waffle maker.
7. Cook for 4 minutes.
8. Open and let waffle cook for 2 minutes.
9. Add the remaining batter to the device and repeat the steps.

Nutritional Value:

- Calories 166
- Total Fat 9.5g
- Saturated Fat 4.3g
- Cholesterol 99mg
- Sodium 99mg
- Potassium 305mg
- Total Carbohydrate 3.7g
- Dietary Fiber 1g
- Protein 5.6g

91. Banana Nut Muffin

Preparation Time: 10 minutes

Cooking Time: 12 minutes

Servings: 3-4

Ingredients:

- 1 egg
- 1 oz. cream cheese
- ¼ cup mozzarella cheese, shredded
- 1 teaspoon banana extract
- 2 tablespoons sweetener
- 1 teaspoon baking powder
- 4 tablespoons almond flour
- 2 tablespoons walnuts, chopped

Method:

1. Combine all the ingredients in a bowl.
2. Turn on the waffle maker.
3. Add the batter to the waffle maker.
4. Seal and cook for 4 minutes.
5. Open and transfer the waffle to a plate. Let cool for 2 minutes.
6. Do the same steps with the remaining mixture.

Nutritional Value:

- Calories 169
- Total Fat 14g
- Saturated Fat 4.6g
- Cholesterol 99mg
- Sodium 98mg
- Potassium 343mg
- Total Carbohydrate 5.6g
- Dietary Fiber 2g
- Protein 7.5g
- Total Sugars 0.6g

92. Pizza Flavored Chaffle

Preparation Time: 10 minutes

Cooking Time: 12 minutes

Servings: 3

Ingredients:

- 1 egg, beaten
- ½ cup cheddar cheese, shredded
- 2 tablespoons pepperoni, chopped
- 1 tablespoon keto marinara sauce
- 4 tablespoons almond flour
- 1 teaspoon baking powder
- ½ teaspoon dried Italian seasoning
- Parmesan cheese, grated

Method:

1. Preheat your waffle maker.
2. In a bowl, mix the egg, cheddar cheese, pepperoni, marinara sauce, almond flour, baking powder and Italian seasoning.
3. Add the mixture to the waffle maker.
4. Close the device and cook for 4 minutes.
5. Open it and transfer chaffle to a plate.
6. Let cool for 2 minutes.
7. Repeat the steps with the remaining batter.
8. Top with the grated Parmesan and serve.

Nutritional Value:

- Calories 179
- Total Fat 14.3g
- Saturated Fat 7.5g
- Cholesterol 118mg
- Sodium 300mg
- Potassium 326mg
- Total Carbohydrate 1.8g
- Dietary Fiber 0.1g
- Protein 11.1g
- Total Sugars 0.4g

93. Chocolate Chaffle

Preparation Time: 5 minutes

Cooking Time: 8 minutes

Servings: 2

Ingredients:

- 1 egg
- ½ cup mozzarella cheese, shredded
- ½ teaspoon baking powder
- 2 tablespoons cocoa powder
- 2 tablespoons sweetener
- 2 tablespoons almond flour

Method:

1. Turn your waffle maker on.
2. Beat the egg in a bowl.
3. Stir in the rest of the ingredients.
4. Put the mixture into the waffle maker.
5. Seal the device and cook for 4 minutes.
6. Open and transfer the chaffle to a plate to cool for 2 minutes.
7. Do the same steps using the remaining mixture.

Nutritional Value:

- Calories 149
- Total Fat 10.8g
- Saturated Fat 2.4g
- Cholesterol 86mg
- Sodium 80mg
- Potassium 291mg
- Total Carbohydrate 9g
- Dietary Fiber 4.1g
- Protein 8.8g
- Total Sugars 0.3g

94. Maple Syrup & Vanilla Chaffle

Preparation Time: 10 minutes

Cooking Time: 12 minutes

Servings: 3

Ingredients:

- 1 egg, beaten
- ¼ cup mozzarella cheese, shredded
- 1 oz. cream cheese
- 1 teaspoon vanilla
- 1 tablespoon keto maple syrup
- 1 teaspoon sweetener
- 1 teaspoon baking powder
- 4 tablespoons almond flour

Method:

1. Preheat your waffle maker.
2. Add all the ingredients to a bowl.
3. Mix well.
4. Pour some of the batter into the waffle maker.
5. Cover and cook for 4 minutes.
6. Transfer chaffle to a plate and let cool for 2 minutes.
7. Repeat the same process with the remaining mixture.

Nutritional Value:

- Calories 146
- Total Fat 9.5g
- Saturated Fat 4.3g
- Cholesterol 99mg
- Potassium 322mg
- Sodium 99mg
- Total Carbohydrate 10.6g
- Dietary Fiber 0.9g
- Protein 5.6g
- Total Sugars 6.4g

95. Red Velvet Chaffle

Preparation Time: 5 minutes

Cooking Time: 12 minutes

Servings: 3

Ingredients:

- 1 egg
- ¼ cup mozzarella cheese, shredded
- 1 oz. cream cheese
- 4 tablespoons almond flour
- 1 teaspoon baking powder
- 2 teaspoons sweetener
- 1 teaspoon red velvet extract
- 2 tablespoons cocoa powder

Method:

1. Combine all the ingredients in a bowl.
2. Plug in your waffle maker.
3. Pour some of the batter into the waffle maker.
4. Seal and cook for 4 minutes.
5. Open and transfer to a plate.
6. Repeat the steps with the remaining batter.

Nutritional Value:

- Calories 126
- Total Fat 10.1g
- Saturated Fat 3.4g
- Cholesterol 66mg
- Sodium 68mg
- Potassium 290mg
- Total Carbohydrate 6.5g
- Dietary Fiber 2.8g
- Protein 5.9g
- Total Sugars 0.2g

96. Chaffle Tortilla

Preparation Time: 5 minutes

Cooking Time: 8 minutes

Servings: 2

Ingredients:

- 1 egg
- ½ cup cheddar cheese, shredded
- 1 teaspoon baking powder
- 4 tablespoons almond flour
- ¼ teaspoon garlic powder
- 1 tablespoon almond milk
- Homemade salsa
- Sour cream
- Jalapeno pepper, chopped

Method:

1. Preheat your waffle maker.
2. Beat the egg in a bowl.
3. Stir in the cheese, baking powder, flour, garlic powder and almond milk.
4. Pour half of the batter into the waffle maker.
5. Cover and cook for 4 minutes.
6. Open and transfer to a plate. Let cool for 2 minutes.
7. Do the same for the remaining batter.
8. Top the waffle with salsa, sour cream and jalapeno pepper.
9. Roll the waffle.

Nutritional Value:

- Calories 225
- Total Fat 17.6g
- Saturated Fat 9.9g
- Cholesterol 117mg
- Sodium 367mg
- Potassium 366mg
- Total Carbohydrate 6g
- Dietary Fiber 0.8g
- Protein 11.3g
- Total Sugars 1.9g

97. Churro Chaffle

Preparation Time: 5 minutes

Cooking Time: 8 minutes

Servings: 2

Ingredients:

- 1 egg
- ½ cup mozzarella cheese, shredded
- ½ teaspoon cinnamon
- 2 tablespoons sweetener

Method:

1. Turn on your waffle iron.
2. Beat the egg in a bowl.
3. Stir in the cheese.
4. Pour half of the mixture into the waffle maker.
5. Cover the waffle iron.
6. Cook for 4 minutes.
7. While waiting, mix the cinnamon and sweetener in a bowl.
8. Open the device and soak the waffle in the cinnamon mixture.
9. Repeat the steps with the remaining batter.

Nutritional Value:

- Calories 106
- Total Fat 6.9g
- Saturated Fat 2.9g
- Cholesterol 171mg
- Sodium 147mg
- Potassium 64mg
- Total Carbohydrate 5.8g
- Dietary Fiber 2.6g
- Protein 9.6g
- Total Sugars 0.4g

98. Chocolate Chip Chaffle

Preparation Time: 5 minutes

Cooking Time: 8 minutes

Servings: 2

Ingredients:

- 1 egg
- ½ teaspoon coconut flour
- ¼ teaspoon baking powder
- 1 teaspoon sweetener
- 1 tablespoon heavy whipping cream
- 1 tablespoon chocolate chips

Method:

1. Preheat your waffle maker.
2. Beat the egg in a bowl.
3. Stir in the flour, baking powder, sweetener and cream.
4. Pour half of the mixture into the waffle maker.
5. Sprinkle the chocolate chips on top and close.
6. Cook for 4 minutes.
7. Remove the chaffle and put on a plate.
8. Do the same procedure with the remaining batter.

Nutritional Value:

- Calories 146
- Total Fat 10 g
- Saturated Fat 7 g
- Cholesterol 88 mg
- Sodium 140 mg
- Potassium 50 mg
- Total Carbohydrate 5 g
- Dietary Fiber 3 g
- Protein 6 g
- Total Sugars 1 g

99. Breakfast Chaffle Sandwich

Preparation Time: 10 minutes

Cooking Time: 10 minutes

Serving: 1

Ingredients:

- 2 basics cooked chaffles
- Cooking spray
- 2 slices bacon
- 1 egg

Method:

1. Spray your pan with oil.
2. Place it over medium heat.
3. Cook the bacon until golden and crispy.
4. Put the bacon on top of one chaffle.
5. In the same pan, cook the egg without mixing until the yolk is set.
6. Add the egg on top of the bacon.
7. Top with another chaffle.

Nutritional Value:

- Calories 514
- Total Fat 47 g
- Saturated Fat 27 g
- Cholesterol 274 mg
- Sodium 565 mg
- Potassium 106 mg
- Total Carbohydrate 2 g
- Dietary Fiber 1 g
- Protein 21 g
- Total Sugars 1 g

100. Sausage & Egg Chaffle Sandwich

Preparation Time: 5 minutes

Cooking Time: 10 minutes

Serving: 1

Ingredients:

- 2 basics cooked chaffles
- 1 tablespoon olive oil
- 1 sausage, sliced into rounds
- 1 egg

Method:

1. Pour olive oil into your pan over medium heat.
2. Put it over medium heat.
3. Add the sausage and cook until brown on both sides.
4. Put the sausage rounds on top of one chaffle.
5. Cook the egg in the same pan without mixing.
6. Place on top of the sausage rounds.
7. Top with another chaffle.

Nutritional Value:

- Calories 332
- Total Fat 21.6g
- Saturated Fat 4.4g
- Cholesterol 139mg
- Potassium 168mg
- Sodium 463mg
- Total Carbohydrate 24.9g
- Dietary Fiber 0g
- Protein 10g
- Total Sugars 0.2g

101. Bacon, Egg & Avocado Chaffle Sandwich

Preparation Time: 5 minutes

Cooking Time: 10 minutes

Servings: 2

Ingredients:

- Cooking spray
- 4 slices bacon
- 2 eggs
- ½ avocado, mashed
- 4 basic chaffles
- 2 leaves lettuce

Method:

1. Coat your skillet with cooking spray.
2. Cook the bacon until golden and crisp.
3. Transfer into a paper towel lined plate.
4. Crack the eggs into the same pan and cook until firm.
5. Flip and cook until the yolk is set.
6. Spread the avocado on the chaffle.
7. Top with lettuce, egg and bacon.
8. Top with another chaffle.

Nutritional Value:

- Calories 372
- Total Fat 30.1g
- Saturated Fat 8.6g
- Cholesterol 205mg
- Sodium 943mg
- Total Carbohydrate 5.4g
- Dietary Fiber 3.4g
- Total Sugars 0.6g
- Protein 20.6g
- Potassium 524mg

102. Pumpkin Chaffles with Choco Chips

Preparation Time: 5 minutes

Cooking Time: 12 minutes

Servings: 3

Ingredients:

- 1 egg
- ½ cup shredded mozzarella cheese
- 4 teaspoons pureed pumpkin
- ¼ teaspoon pumpkin pie spice
- 2 tablespoons sweetener
- 1 tablespoon almond flour
- 4 teaspoons chocolate chips (sugar-free)

Method:

1. Turn your waffle maker on.
2. In a bowl, beat the egg and stir in the pureed pumpkin.
3. Mix well.
4. Add the rest of the ingredients one by one.
5. Pour 1/3 of the mixture to your waffle maker.
6. Cook for 4 minutes.
7. Repeat the same steps with the remaining mixture.

Nutritional Value:

- Calories 93
- Total Fat 7 g
- Saturated Fat 3 g
- Cholesterol 69 mg
- Sodium 138 mg
- Potassium 48 mg
- Total Carbohydrate 2 g
- Dietary Fiber 1 g
- Protein 7 g
- Total Sugars 1 g

103. Choco Waffle with Cream Cheese

Preparation Time: 5 minutes

Cooking Time: 8 minutes

Servings: 2

Ingredients:

Choco Chaffle

- 2 tablespoons cocoa powder
- 1 tablespoon almond flour
- ¼ teaspoon baking powder
- 2 tablespoons sweetener
- 1 egg, beaten
- ½ teaspoon vanilla extract
- 1 tablespoon heavy whipping cream

Frosting

- 2 tablespoons cream cheese
- 2 teaspoons confectioner's sugar (swerve)
- 1/8 teaspoon vanilla extract
- 1 teaspoon heavy cream

Method:

1. Combine all the choco chaffle ingredients in a large bowl, adding the wet ingredients last.
2. Mix well.
3. Plug in your waffle maker.
4. Pour half of the mixture into the device.
5. Close and cook for 4 minutes.
6. Cook the other waffle.
7. While waiting, make your frosting by adding cream cheese to a heat proof bowl.
8. Place in the microwave.
9. Microwave for 8 seconds.
10. Use a mixer to blend the cream cheese with the rest of the frosting ingredients.

11. Process until fluffy.

12. Spread the frosting on top of the chaffle.

13. Put another chaffle on top.

14. Pipe the rest of the frosting on top of the chaffle.

15. **Slice and serve.**

Nutritional Value:

- Calories 151
- Total Fat 13 g
- Saturated Fat 6 g
- Cholesterol 111 mg
- Sodium 83 mg
- Potassium 190 mg
- Total Carbohydrate 5 g
- Dietary Fiber 2 g
- Protein 6 g
- Total Sugars 1 g

104. Open-Faced Ham & Green Bell Pepper Chaffle Sandwich

Preparation Time: 10 minutes

Cooking Time: 10 minutes

Servings: 2

Ingredients:

- 2 slices ham
- Cooking spray
- 1 green bell pepper, sliced into strips
- 2 slices cheese
- 1 tablespoon black olives, pitted and sliced
- 2 basic chaffles

Method:

1. Cook the ham in a pan coated with oil over medium heat.
2. Next, cook the bell pepper.
3. Assemble the open-faced sandwich by topping each chaffle with ham and cheese, bell pepper and olives.
4. Toast in the oven until the cheese has melted a little.

Nutritional Value:

- Calories 365
- Total Fat 24.6g
- Saturated Fat 13.6g
- Cholesterol 91mg
- Sodium 1154mg
- Potassium 440mg
- Total Carbohydrate 8g
- Dietary Fiber 2.6g
- Protein 24.5g
- Total Sugars 6.3g

105. Sausage & Pepperoni Chaffle Sandwich

Preparation Time: 10 minutes

Cooking Time: 10 minutes

Servings: 4

Ingredients:

- Cooking spray
- 2 cervelat sausage, sliced into rounds
- 12 pieces pepperoni
- 6 mushroom slices
- 4 teaspoons mayonnaise
- 4 big white onion rings
- 4 basic chaffles

Method:

1. Spray your skillet with oil.
2. Place over medium heat.
3. Cook the sausage until brown on both sides.
4. Transfer on a plate.
5. Cook the pepperoni and mushrooms for 2 minutes.
6. Spread mayo on top of the chaffle.
7. Top with the sausage, pepperoni, mushrooms and onion rings.
8. Top with another chaffle.

Nutritional Value:

- Calories 373
- Total Fat 24.4g
- Saturated Fat 6g
- Cholesterol 27mg
- Sodium 717mg
- Potassium 105mg
- Total Carbohydrate 29.8g
- Dietary Fiber 1.1g
- Protein 8.1g
- Total Sugars 4.5g

106. Mini Keto Pizza

Preparation Time: 10 minutes

Cooking Time: 15 minutes

Servings: 2

Ingredients:

- 1 egg
- ½ cup mozzarella cheese, shredded
- ¼ teaspoon basil
- ¼ teaspoon garlic powder
- 1 tablespoon almond flour
- ½ teaspoon baking powder
- 2 tablespoons reduced-carb pasta sauce
- 2 tablespoons mozzarella cheese

Method:

1. Preheat your waffle maker.
2. In a bowl, beat the egg.
3. Stir in the ½ cup mozzarella cheese, basil, garlic powder, almond flour and baking powder.
4. Add half of the mixture to your waffle maker.
5. Cook for 4 minutes.
6. Transfer to a baking sheet.
7. Cook the second mini pizza.
8. While both pizzas are on the baking sheet, spread the pasta sauce on top.
9. Sprinkle the cheese on top.
10. Bake in the oven until the cheese has melted.

Nutritional Value:

- Calories 195
- Total Fat 14 g
- Saturated Fat 6 g
- Cholesterol 116 mg
- Sodium 301 mg
- Potassium 178 mg
- Total Carbohydrate 4 g
- Dietary Fiber 1 g
- Protein 13 g
- Total Sugars 1 g

107. Pumkpin Chaffle with Maple Syrup

Preparation Time: 5 minutes

Cooking Time: 16 minutes

Servings: 2

Ingredients:

- 2 eggs, beaten
- ½ cup mozzarella cheese, shredded
- 1 teaspoon coconut flour
- ¾ teaspoon baking powder
- ¾ teaspoon pumpkin pie spice
- 2 teaspoons pureed pumpkin
- 4 teaspoons heavy whipping cream
- ½ teaspoon vanilla
- Pinch salt
- 2 teaspoons maple syrup (sugar-free)

Method:

1. Turn your waffle maker on.
2. Mix all the ingredients except maple syrup in a large bowl.
3. Pour half of the batter into the waffle maker.
4. Close and cook for 4 minutes.
5. Transfer to a plate to cool for 2 minutes.
6. Repeat the steps with the remaining mixture.
7. Drizzle the maple syrup on top of the chaffles before serving.

Nutritional Value:

- Calories 201
- Total Fat 15 g
- Saturated Fat 8 g
- Cholesterol 200 mg
- Sodium 249 mg
- Potassium 271 mg
- Total Carbohydrate 4 g
- Dietary Fiber 1 g
- Protein 12 g
- Total Sugars 1 g

108. Swiss Bacon Chaffle

Preparation Time: 5 minutes

Cooking Time: 8 minutes

Servings: 2

Ingredients:

- 1 egg
- ½ cup Swiss cheese
- 2 tablespoons cooked crumbled bacon

Method:

1. Preheat your waffle maker.
2. Beat the egg in a bowl.
3. Stir in the cheese and bacon.
4. Pour half of the mixture into the device.
5. Close and cook for 4 minutes.
6. Cook the second chaffle using the same steps.

Nutritional Value:

- Calories 237
- Total Fat 17.6g
- Saturated Fat 8.1g
- Cholesterol 128mg
- Sodium 522mg
- Total Carbohydrate 1.9g
- Dietary Fiber 0g
- Total Sugars 0.5g
- Protein 17.1g
- Potassium 158mg

109. Bacon, Olives & Cheddar Chaffle

Preparation Time: 5 minutes

Cooking Time: 8 minutes

Servings: 2

Ingredients:

- 1 egg
- ½ cup cheddar cheese, shredded
- 1 tablespoon black olives, chopped
- 1 tablespoon bacon bits

Method:

1. Plug in your waffle maker.
2. In a bowl, beat the egg and stir in the cheese.
3. Add the black olives and bacon bits.
4. Mix well.
5. Add half of the mixture into the waffle maker.
6. Cover and cook for 4 minutes.
7. Open and transfer to a plate.
8. Let cool for 2 minutes.
9. Cook the other chaffle using the remaining batter.

Nutritional Value:

- Calories 202
- Total Fat 16g
- Saturated Fat 8g
- Cholesterol 122mg
- Sodium 462mg
- Potassium 111mg
- Total Carbohydrate 0.9g
- Dietary Fiber 0.1g
- Protein 13.4g
- Total Sugars 0.3g

SHOPPING LIST

Pepper

Salt

Yellow onion

Eggs

Cauliflower

Mixed berries

Vanilla extract

Almond extract

Sweetener

Cream cheese

Cottage cheese

Cheddar cheese

Sugar-free barbecue sauce

Bacon

Ground beef

Parmesan cheese, grated

Almond flour

Onion powder

Garlic powder

Cauliflower crumbles

Eggs

Coconut

Pumpkin seeds

Blueberries

Butter

Dried oregano

Mozzarella

Black olives

Turkey pepperoni

Grape tomatoes

Olive oil

Cinnamon

Herbed goat cheese

Ground pork

Ground beef

Water

Whiskey

Bacon grease

Apple cider vinegar

Mayonnaise

Green onions

Red cabbage

Toothpicks

Alfalfa sprouts

Coriander

Honey

Tamari Soy Sauce

Fish Sauce

Honey

Chile garlic sauce

Fat coconut milk

Peanut butter

Swiss cheese

Mayonnaise

Dijon mustard

Sauerkraut

Corned beef

Dijon mustard

Dry thyme

Spinach

Carrots

Mushrooms

Pork

Onion	shrimp	Strawberries
Sesame seeds	Water	Stevia
Lemon juice	Flaxseeds	Coconut flakes
Onion	Coconut Oil	Paprika
Olive Oil	Baking Powder	Blueberries
Parsley	Carrot	Banana
chicken	Avocado	Almond milk
beef	Lemon juice	Tomatoes
pork	Ginger	Broccoli

CONCLUSION

There are not many moments in life when we feel that we can actually make a change in the world, especially when there are so many large corporations that seem to be taking over everything. But surprisingly, by preparing your own food, you are actually standing up for yourself and not purchasing something that was produced only to suit the masses, and not something that was made to actually provide you with nutrition. Stand up for yourself and your loved ones by making chaffle something that you will prepare on your own, without being overcome by the large corporations.

There are several popular alternatives to grain flour that are appropriate for a ketogenic diet. Perhaps the most frequently relied upon low carb substitutes for refined high-carbohydrate flour are coconut and almond flour as well as psyllium husk powder.

With these recipes at your fingertips, you don't need to let anything between you and weight loss success with a ketogenic diet!

As you can see, there are countless possibilities when it comes to making low carb cheese waffles.

And because these are a cinch to make, you don't have to worry about spending a long time inside the kitchen.

You can make a pair of chaffles in as quickly as 10 minutes. You can even freeze the batter in advance so you can save time and effort preparing your breakfast or snack.

Made in the USA
Monee, IL
01 February 2020